D0523267

5 minutes

TO A GREAT

REAL ESTATE

LETTER

A DESK REFERENCE FOR TOP-SELLING AGENTS

JOHN D. MAYFIELD

ABR®, ABRM, GRI, e-PRO®, CRB

THOMSON
★
SOUTH-WESTERN

Australia · Canada · Mexico · Singapore · Spain · United Kingdom · United States

THOMSON
★
™
SOUTH-WESTERN

5 Minutes to a Great Real Estate Letter: A Desk Reference for Top-Selling Agents

John D. Mayfield

VP/Editorial Director:
Jack W. Calhoun

VP/Editor-in-Chief:
Dave Shaut

Executive Editor:
Scott Person

Developmental Editor:
Sara Froelicher

Marketing Manager:
Mark Linton

Production Manager:
Barbara Fuller Jacobsen

Sr. Technology Project Manager:
Matt McKinney

Manufacturing Coordinator:
Charlene Taylor

Production House/Compositor:
DPS Associates

Printer:
Thomson West
Eagan, Minnesota

Art Director:
Chris A. Miller

Internal Designer:
Erwin Swillinger
DPS Associates

ASIA (including India)
Thomson Learning
5 Shenton Way
#01-01 UIC Building
Singapore 068808

CANADA
Thomson Nelson
1120 Birchmount Road
Toronto, Ontario
Canada M1K 5G4

AUSTRALIA/NEW ZEALAND
Thomson Learning Australia
102 Dodds Street
Southbank, Victoria 3006
Australia

UK/EUROPE/MIDDLE
EAST/AFRICA
Thomson Learning
High Holborn House
50-51 Bedford Road
London WC1R 4LR
United Kingdom

LATIN AMERICA
Thomson Learning
Seneca, 53
Colonia Polanco
11560 Mexico
D.F.Mexico

SPAIN (includes Portugal)
Thomson Paraninfo
Calle Magallanes, 25
28015 Madrid, Spain

Dedication

To my wife, Kerry. She has always been such an inspiration and help to me. I truly would not have the joy and enthusiasm I have for this career in real estate if it were not for her. Thank you Kerry for being such a special and wonderful person in my life, and most of all for being a great wife!

Epigraph

It makes little difference how many university courses or degrees a person may own. If he cannot use words to move an idea from one point to another, his education is incomplete.

—Norman Cousins (1912–1990),
U.S. essayist, editor, *Saturday Review*

Contents

Please note: There are additional letters, e-mail messages, fax templates, and other resources provided on the CD-ROM.

Foreword

5 Minutes to a Great Real Estate Letter contains numerous ideas for real estate agents and brokers to use to correspond with the public, clients, and customers. John Mayfield gives you the tools to use in an easy to understand format.

Each day you have a precious commodity to market—YOU! Don't forget YOU are valuable and must market your services with integrity to the public, clients, and customers. *5 Minutes to a Great Real Estate Letter* will allow you to correspond and communicate effectively and efficiently with everyone you come in contact with. You will improve your communication skills, save time and money, and at the same time, your correspondence will be more professional. John cares about people and this is shown as he shares his comprehensive knowledge of the subject matter.

I have personally worked with John through the Missouri Association of REALTORS®, and I can attest that John believes in correspondence and communication. I have worked closely with John as one of MAR's GRI instructors. He is knowledgeable and proficient on this subject matter. He uses his experience in real estate to help you as a person and to improve your business.

I encourage you to use this book and CD in several ways. First, learn how to communicate effectively and efficiently with everyone you come into contact with by using the correspondence in this book. Change and edit the correspondence to fit your personality and your marketing area. Second, put John's innovative ideas and methods to work immediately. Your customers will see how professional your correspondence looks and realize you are keeping in touch. Finally, these ideas will save you time and money. Your time will not be wasted and your correspondence and communication will help improve your business. Choose the correspondence and methods that work best for you and customize them.

The best part is to realize that with John's help, you are only *5 Minutes to a Great Real Estate Letter*!

—Terry Murphy
National Association of REALTORS®
Chair of State Education Directors, 2003

Introduction

Over my 26 plus years of selling real estate, I have met with many colleagues and have noticed both positive and negative work habits in this group of friends. During my real estate seminars, I like to explain that I have walked around in the "real estate laboratory" watching and noting ideas that have worked and/or failed over this duration. Please do not misunderstand me—just because something does not work one day or one year does not mean it will never work. People should always be willing to try new ideas regardless of the previous outcome. However, one item I have noticed that is important for all of us, no matter what business we are in, is our communication and appearance to the consumer. People will decide if they like you in the first minute or two of a meeting. Much of this, I believe, revolves around our appearance and how well we communicate with the client. This appearance measuring stick comes in many forms, and not just in our physical facade. In sales (especially real estate), measurement of our marketing materials for the products we sell daily plays an important part in our business success. What do our brochures and flyers look like? What about our business cards? And, yes, do not forget our daily communication through letters and e-mails!

We normally think of products in the real estate industry as "houses." Yet there is another product you and I must sell every day in our marketplace: Ourselves! That is right, do not forget that *you* are a product, too. Marketing yourself to buyers and sellers is essential and requires your daily attention. Unfortunately, most real estate agents forget about this and fail to realize how poorly they market the most important product they sell every day.

Do you realize that every time you send out a piece of correspondence to a client or customer, it has your résumé on it? Every follow-up letter, every proposal to a consumer, each "thank you" note, even memos, faxes, and e-mail messages reveal an image of you.

In this so-called "real estate laboratory" that I described in the first paragraph, I've observed that the portrayal of an agent's image through his or her correspondence is, often, not done well. I have witnessed many whom do not have the necessary typing skills, let alone know how to format a good business letter, or what a full block letter format is all about. Agents have sent me notes and letters in their own handwriting that were almost scary when I first viewed them. I do not want to belittle my colleagues. I only want them to realize that if their correspondence left a negative impression on me, the same was probably true of the consumer, too.

There are three main goals of this book. The first is to help real estate agents and brokers improve their communication skills through letters, faxes, and e-mails to the public, clients and customers, other real estate agents, and various vendors we come into contact with each day.

The second goal of this book is to help save you time! I understand how hectic and busy our business has become. The need to save time by taking a shortcut in corresponding with a client confronts us daily. With *5 Minutes to a Great Real Estate Letter,* you can look professional through your written communication without sacrificing much time.

The final objective of this book is to get you to use the letters! I've tried to make the letters and notes look and sound professional, and able to fit a multitude of personality styles. Keep in mind that you are free to edit and change anything you like to make the correspondence sound like you.

In closing, if I asked you what the number one complaint most consumers (especially sellers) have about their real estate agent is, what would you guess? That's right, the lack of communication they received from their agent. *"We never heard a word from our agent"* is the common phrase I hear when listing a property previously listed by another firm. More and more real estate agents fail to understand how important staying in touch with their clients and customers on a consistent basis is. With *5 Minutes to a Great Real Estate Letter,* you can stay in touch with people you are working with, and look professional, without the expense of much time.

Good luck, and "thanks" for buying the book!

Acknowledgments

I owe a special thank you to my real estate agents and staff at Mayfield Real Estate, Inc. Special thanks to Mary Langston, Paul Pinkston, Lyle Laughman, Pam Oder, Fredi Holbert, David Goldsmith, Esta Lea Cissell, Donna Earhart, and Susie McBride for their input on my letters and the book. Thanks to Zac McDowell and my friends and assistants Amanda Herzog and Angie Hagerty. Thanks to my editor, Sara Froelicher, and everyone else at Thomson Business and Professional Publishing.

I am always indebted to my two daughters, Alyx and Anne Mayfield, who encourage and allow Dad the opportunity to work so hard on his projects. Thank you to my Mother, Pat Mayfield, who introduced me to the field of real estate, for all of the guidance and direction she provided to me. Thanks Mom!

And finally, thank you to my wife Kerry, my best friend!

How to Use This Book

You can use Microsoft® Word and Outlook with *5 Minutes to a Great Real Estate Letter*. However, you do not need to have these software products to use the letters on the CD-ROM. Included on the CD-ROM are .txt files that you can import into whatever word processing program you use, as most softwares allow for this feature. Because .txt files are generic in nature, many letters throughout the book that uses italic or bold font styles will not show those styles in the .txt format for those programs. You will need to add some of these font styles yourself, and then save the file on your computer hard drive. You can watch a short viewlet entitled "Converting and customizing .txt files" included on the CD-ROM.

You will notice various letters throughout the book that contain more personalization. Those letters will need your manual input to make the letters work properly. Below is an example:

> For a *"FREE"* price evaluation of what your property is worth in today's market, call me at *[Agent Phone Number]*. There are no high-pressure tactics and no obligation to list your house.

In the example, you will need to add your phone number to the paragraph for this letter to be ready for mailing. Once you make the necessary changes and save your letter to your computer hard drive, it is ready for reuse to other clients without this extra step. You can watch a short viewlet entitled "Making Changes and Customizing Your Letters" included on the CD-ROM.

One often asked question is, "Can I change the letters to suit my writing style?" The answer is yes! All the letters are easily editable, and a demonstration of this is also available on the CD-ROM. There is even a demonstration on how you can add letters to the existing letter library for future use.

All note card letters work with Avery Item #3379, note card size 4¼ x 5½. Although the note card templates can be used with your computer and most printers, you can also use these templates to handwrite your notes, adding that personal touch.

The e-mail messages on the CD-ROM are in Word and .txt files. A viewlet on the CD-ROM explains several ways to use these messages for fast and easy retrieval, so you are never more than "5 Minutes from Sending a Great Real Estate Letter."

One final note. Every attempt has been made to make the letters and viewlets on the CD-ROM match the existing step-by-step procedures currently used in Microsoft® Office. If this information or keystrokes change with a new software upgrade by Microsoft®, please check http://www.5-Minutes.com to watch the latest viewlets for use with the letters and e-mail messages from the book.

Prospecting

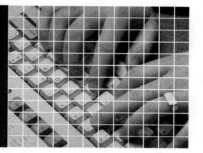

Author, speaker, and motivator Stephen R. Covey said, "The only thing that endures over time is the 'Law of the Farm.' You must prepare the ground, plant the seed, cultivate, and water if you expect to reap the harvest." Covey's words strike a chord for the salespersons of our world; if you don't prospect, there will be no reward to harvest!

As with any form of prospecting, personal contact is always best. Studies show that communication is most effective through our facial expressions and tone of voice. Only a small fraction of the words we use are helpful in developing rapport with clients and customers. It is best to make a personal visit or contact when prospecting any time you can; however, keep the no-call rules and guidelines for your state available so you will not break any laws on this subject.

With the no-call rules in place, using direct mail for prospecting is a great way to build your business. This book contains a large selection of letters for use with your daily prospecting. Feel free to edit and change any of the letters in the book to fit your style of writing. The key to using the prospecting letters in this book is to be consistent with your prospecting! If you send one or two letters and nothing happens, don't give up. If you do a mass mailing of one or two hundred letters and nothing happens, don't give up.

Prospecting is what it means: "prospecting!" It is a daily routine that is a must for any salesperson to be successful. Have fun using the letters, try to

make a personal contact when possible, and remember Mr. Covey's "Law of the Farm." Keep tilling the ground and don't forget to water it daily. When you consistently follow these guidelines, you will surely reap the harvest!

Expired Listing #1

[Date]

«AddressBlock»

«GreetingLine»

Hi, my name is *[Agent's Name]*, and I noticed your listing recently expired from our Multiple Listing Service® (MLS®). Unfortunately, this means that your property does not appear in any computer searches other real estate agents use when working with potential buyers in your price range.

If you're still interested in selling your property, I would love to visit with you and explain some of my marketing ideas that have been successful for many of my clients. I have enclosed a sample flyer and a postcard that I use in my marketing campaigns for new listings.

If I can help in any way, please give me a call. I hope to hear from you soon.

Sincerely,

[Agent Name]
[Agent Title]

Please void this offer if your property is currently listed with another real estate broker.

Expired Listing #2

[Date]

«AddressBlock»

«GreetingLine»

Hi, my name is *[Agent's Name]*, and I noticed your real estate listing recently expired from our Multiple Listing Service® (MLS®). Unfortunately, this means that your property will not appear in any computer searches other real estate agents use when working with potential buyers in your price range.

May I ask you two questions?

- ☐ *Are you still interested in selling your real estate?*
- ☐ *Do you feel a fresh start with another real estate agency might be helpful in selling your home?*

If you checked either box above, then perhaps I could help jump-start your marketing efforts for the coming weeks. I would love to visit with you and show you some of the marketing strategies I use in selling properties.

For this FREE, no obligation consultation, please call me today. I appreciate your time, and I hope to hear from you soon.

Sincerely,

[Agent Name]
[Agent Title]

Please void this offer if your property is currently listed with another real estate broker.

Expired Listing #3

[Date]

«AddressBlock»

«GreetingLine»

Hi, my name is *[Agent's Name]*. I noticed you had your house for sale recently, and I was wondering if you still had an interest in selling. I have a unique marketing plan I would love to share with you, and some other ideas I feel may be of benefit in helping to sell your property.

Now is a great time to buy and sell a home! For a FREE price evaluation on what your property is worth on today's real estate market, call me at *[Agent's Phone Number]*. There is no pressure or contract to buy or sell through me, and the entire process does not take long.

I appreciate your time, and I hope to hear from you soon.

Yours truly,

[Agent Name]
[Agent Title]

Please void this offer if your property is currently listed with another real estate broker.

Expired Listing #4

[Date]

«AddressBlock»

«GreetingLine»

Hi, my name is *[Agent's Name]*. I realize your house did not sell while listed through our Multiple Listing Service®, but don't let this discourage you; there may be a good reason. Sometimes a fresh start with a different real estate company makes all the difference in the world. I would love to visit with you and explain some marketing ideas I use and give you my feedback on what would help to sell your house.

Call me at *[Agent's Phone Number]* if this sounds like something you're interested in. Please understand there is no obligation to buy or sell through me. I promise not to take up much of your time and, yes, it is absolutely FREE!

I appreciate your time and I hope to hear from you soon.

Sincerely,

[Agent Name]
[Agent Title]

Please void this offer if your property is currently listed with another real estate broker.

Expired Listing—Follow-Up #1

[Date]

«AddressBlock»

«GreetingLine»

I hope you received my letter a couple of weeks ago. I noticed your property listing is still missing from our local Multiple Listing Service®, which normally means one of several things:

1. You have decided not to sell.
2. You have already sold your home. If so, congratulations!
3. You have re-listed, and this letter crossed in the mail with reentering your listing in our Multiple Listing Service®.
4. You are still debating what to do about the sale of your house.
5. And, of course, other circumstances and situations may exist that are holding up the marketing efforts of your house.

If you are still considering selling your real estate, please keep me in mind to discuss some ideas I have for selling your property. I would love to visit with you on this matter.

Thank you for your time.

Sincerely,

[Agent Name]
[Agent Title]

Please void this offer if your property is currently listed with another real estate broker.

[Date]

«AddressBlock»

«GreetingLine»

I hope you had a chance to review the information I left at your house recently, and I trust you found it helpful. I understand your preference to sell your property on your own, and, to help you with this, I am making available for you to borrow a video called *"Preparing Your Home For Show,"* by David Knox Productions. This is an excellent program which points out information you should know and steps to complete to help get top dollar for your property.

I would also like to offer you an opportunity for a free price evaluation on your property to help you to find out what it's worth on today's real estate market.

To borrow the video or for the FREE price evaluation, call me, *[Agent's Name]*, at *[Phone Number]*. There is no pressure or obligation to list or sell through me or my company.

Again, thanks for your time, and please call me if I can help in any way.

Sincerely,

[Agent Name]
[Agent Title]

For Sale by Owner—Follow-Up #2

[Date]

«AddressBlock»

«GreetingLine»

I hope you had a chance to review the information I left at your house recently, and I trust you found it helpful. According to the *2003 National Association of REALTORS® Profile of Home Buyers and Sellers*, the biggest concern among for-sale-by-owners is completing the paperwork. True, there is an enormous amount of forms that need completing to make the transaction run smoothly. This includes everything from the seller's disclosure statement to lead-based paint addenda to occupancy before and after the closing provisions and, of course, the contract itself.

I understand your desire to sell your property on your own, and respect your decision to do so. To help you with this endeavor, I am making available to you sample copies of some of our forms for your attorney to look at and incorporate in your transaction. Unfortunately, I cannot provide you with free forms since our contracts come from our REALTORS® association. However, you are more than welcome to borrow my sample packet if your attorney would want to incorporate some of the same information in his or her sales contract. Let me know if you would like to see this, and I will be glad to drop it by.

I would also like to offer you a price evaluation on your property to determine what it's worth on today's real estate market. This does not take long, and many of my clients find this information helpful during their own marketing efforts.

To use my sample forms packet, or for your price evaluation, call me, *[Agent's Name]*, at *[Phone Number]*. Best of all, they're both FREE, and there is no pressure or duty to list or sell through me or my company.

Again, "thanks" for your time, and please call me if I can help in any way.

Sincerely,

[Agent Name]
[Agent Title]

For Sale by Owner—Follow-Up #3

[Date]

«AddressBlock»

«GreetingLine»

"Thank you" for allowing me to visit with you about the real estate you are selling on your own. I appreciate your kindness and the hospitality, and I wish you the best of luck on your home sale. I have enclosed another business card if you should have any questions during your marketing efforts. Please feel free to call me if you have a concern or question that you would like to discuss.

I have enclosed a sample seller's disclosure (marked **Sample**). You should discuss this form with your attorney before providing it to potential prospects and before entering into a written offer to purchase. Unfortunately, I cannot provide you with a copy of this seller disclosure since this form is for our office transactions only. However, your attorney should be able to prepare a similar document for you to use.

Again, "thanks" for being so kind and generous during my visit. Good luck, and please let me know if I can help in any way.

Sincerely,

[Agent Name]
[Agent Title]

Follow-Up—FSBO with Business Card

[Date]

«AddressBlock»

«GreetingLine»

I wanted to write a short note and thank you for visiting with me this past week about your property for sale. I appreciate your kindness and enjoyed our visit. I have enclosed some business cards with your property photo and a brief description of your real estate for sale. These cards are ideal to give out to friends and co-workers to help spread the word about your house. The key to a successful sale is to create as much interest as possible, and this marketing idea is one good way to carry out that goal. Let me know if you need a few more cards, and I will be glad to print out another sheet for you.

Good luck with your marketing efforts, and if there are any other ideas or suggestions you might want to discuss in marketing your property, feel free to give me a call.

Sincerely,

[Agent Name]
[Agent Title]

FSBO—Lead-Based Paint Disclosure

[Date]

«AddressBlock»

«GreetingLine»

"Thank you" for visiting with me this week about your property for sale. I had mentioned to you the Federal Lead-Based Paint Disclosure Act and promised to send you more information about the law. As I pointed out to you, this is a federal law that requires all sellers, landlords, and agents to disclose to prospective clients information about lead-based paint in housing built before 1978. If your home was built after this date, do not worry about this information. However, if your home was built before 1978, you might want to check out the link below, which will give you the information you need to know about this disclosure. I have copied a short paragraph from the Environmental Protection Agency's web site that shows just how severe this law can be.

What if a seller or lessor fails to comply with these laws?

A seller, lessor, or agent who fails to give the proper information can be sued for triple the amount of damages. In addition, they may be subject to civil and criminal penalties. Ensuring that disclosure information is given to home buyers and tenants helps all parties avoid misunderstandings before, during, and after sales and leasing agreements.

From the EPA Web Site.

My training at *[Agency Name]* allows me to be on top of the latest legal and environmental changes facing sellers such as you. Whenever I can help another individual with this information, I am happy to pass it along. This is important because with lawsuits on the rise in our country, you never know when that next problem about lead-based paint and a failure to disclose could arise right in our own backyard. You can visit the web site listed below and get the proper forms to use when you are ready to prepare a contract for a potential buyer. If you need any more information, please feel free to call me at *[Agent's Phone Number]* or e-mail me at *[Your E-Mail]* and I will be glad to help in any way I can.

http://www.epa.gov/opptintr/lead/leadbase.htm

Thanks for your time, and good luck in selling your home.

Sincerely,

[Agent Name]
[Agent Title]

Thank You—After Knocking on Doors —Might Sell

[Date]

«AddressBlock»

«GreetingLine»

"Thank you" for taking time out to visit with me this week when I was passing out information in your neighborhood. I appreciated your kindness and the hospitality you showed me while I stopped by your house.

You pointed out that you might be in the market to sell your property in the coming months. I want you to feel free to call me if you have a concern or question that you would like to discuss when you are ready to market your property. I would also be glad to provide you with a FREE price evaluation on what your property is worth on today's market. I have enclosed my business card for you to call me when you are ready and I would be happy to provide this free service to you.

Again, "thanks" for being so kind and generous during my visit, and please let me know if I can help in any way.

Sincerely,

[Agent Name]
[Agent Title]

Thank You—After Knocking on Doors

[Date]

«AddressBlock»

«GreetingLine»

"Thank you" for taking time out to visit with me this week when I was passing out information in your neighborhood. I appreciated your kindness and the hospitality you showed me when I stopped by your house.

I wanted to remind you that any time you would like to know what the value of your property is, feel free to call me. It will not take me long to run a search on properties such as yours in our local Multiple Listing Service® (MLS®). You are never under any obligation to buy or sell real estate through me. Best of all, it's FREE!

Again, "thanks" for being so kind and generous during my visit, and please let me know if I can help in any way in the future.

Sincerely,

[Agent Name]
[Agent Title]

Not All Agents Are the Same

[Date]

«AddressBlock»

«GreetingLine»

Did you know all agents are not the same? That's right, not everyone offers the same services or sells real estate in the same way. If you are in the market to buy or sell a home, let me show you how my real estate marketing system is different from that of the average real estate agent.

For a FREE price evaluation of what your property is worth in today's market, call me at [Your Phone Number]. There are no high-pressure tactics and no obligation to list your house with me.

I appreciate your time and I hope to hear from you soon.

Sincerely,

[Agent Name]
[Agent Title]

Open House This Weekend

[Date]

«AddressBlock»

«GreetingLine»

I am holding an open house this weekend in your neighborhood at *[Address of Property]*. If you know of someone who might have an interest in this home, please let that person know about my open house. Viewing will take place on *[Day of Open House]* from *[Time of Open House]*.

Are you interested in selling your house, or would you like to know what its value is on today's real estate market? For a free price evaluation, call me at *[Your Phone Number]*. There are no high-pressure tactics and no obligation to list your house. Best of all, it's FREE!

I appreciate your time, and don't forget my open house this *[Day of Open House]* from *[Time of Open House]*.

Sincerely,

[Agent Name]
[Agent Title]

Owner of Investment Property

[Date]

«AddressBlock»

«GreetingLine»

For the last several weeks, I have been working with some investors looking for property in your area. While researching likely properties, I discovered that you own the *[Type of Investment Property]* at *[Address of Property]* in *[City]*. Have you considered selling your real estate and using the 1031 tax code to exchange for other investment property without paying capital gains tax? If so, I can help you with this transaction.

Please feel free to call me at *[Your Phone Number]* for more information on how you can accomplish this goal and maximize your equity position.

I appreciate your time and hope you will consider this idea.

Yours truly,

[Agent Name]
[Agent Title]

Owner of Vacant Lot

[Date]

«AddressBlock»

«GreetingLine»

Hello, my name is *[Agent's Name]*, and I am a real estate agent with *[Agency Name]*. I noticed that you own a vacant lot at *[Address of Property]* in *[City or Subdivision]*. If you're interested in selling this lot, I would love to help you. Many lots in this area are bringing top dollar, and now is an excellent time to sell.

Call me for a FREE evaluation of what price your lot could command in today's real estate market. I have enclosed my business card for you, if you would like to call me.

I appreciate your time, and I hope to hear from you soon.

Yours truly,

[Agent Name]
[Agent Title]

Vacant House in Neighborhood

[Date]

«AddressBlock»

«GreetingLine»

Hello, my name is *[Agent's Name]*, and I am a real estate agent with *[Agency Name]*. I noticed that you own a house at *[Address of Property]* in *[City]*. Because the property is vacant, I wonder if you might consider selling it? Now is an excellent time to sell real estate, and many of our agents at *[Agency Name]* have potential buyers who cannot find the right home currently for sale through our local Multiple Listing Service®.

If you consider selling this property, please allow me to do a FREE price evaluation for you. There's no pressure to list or sell through my company. I provide this service to many customers who want to know the value of their properties on today's real estate market. It also gives people an opportunity to meet me and learn more about my services so when they are ready to sell they can make an informed decision.

You can visit my web site at *[Web Address]* to learn more about me, and view current listings for sale in your area. I appreciate your time, and again, feel free to call me if I can help in any way.

Sincerely,

[Agent Name]
[Agent Title]

Need Listing in Area or Subdivision

[Date]

«AddressBlock»

«GreetingLine»

Hello, my name is *[Agent's Name]*, with *[Agency Name]*. I am working with some buyers who expressed an interest in a home in your *[Area or Subdivision]*. Are you interested in selling your house? If so, I would be happy to visit with you to discuss what your house is worth on today's real estate market. Best of all, this consultation is FREE, and you are under no obligation to list or sell through me.

Now is a great time to buy or sell real estate!

I appreciate your time. Please call me if you have an interest in selling your house.

Yours truly,

[Agent Name]
[Agent Title]

Just Listed in Neighborhood

[Date]

«AddressBlock»

«GreetingLine»

Hi, my name is [Agent's Name], and I recently listed the real estate at [Listing Address] in your neighborhood. Do you know of some people you would like to have as neighbors? If so, please pass along my business card and a copy of the enclosed flyer to them. I can also arrange a preview of the property for your friends should they decide to look at this lovely home.

Thank you for your time, and if you're ever in the market to know the value of your property, call me for a FREE price evaluation on your house. I'll be glad to provide this information for you.

Sincerely,

[Agent Name]
[Agent Title]

Just Sold #1

[Date]

«AddressBlock»

«GreetingLine»

Hi, my name is *[Agent's Name]*, and I just sold the home at *[Listing Address]* in your neighborhood. Are you considering a move, or, would you just like to know the value of your property? Either way, call me for a FREE price evaluation on what your house might be worth on today's real estate market. I'll be glad to provide this information for you at no cost and no obligation to list.

I hope you'll welcome your new neighbors to the area, and please keep my business card on file if I can help you in any way.

Sincerely,

[Agent Name]
[Agent Title]

Follow-Up after Phone Call to Prospect

[Date]

«AddressBlock»

«GreetingLine»

"Thank you" for taking time out to visit with me on the telephone this week. I appreciate the kindness you showed me when we spoke.

I know that selling your own home can be a rewarding experience, and I wish you the best of luck in marketing your home.

Please know that any time you have questions or concerns about ideas or marketing challenges, I would be happy to help. I also want to remind you that any time you would like to know what the value of your property is compared with other properties currently for sale, I can help with that too! It will not take me long to run a search on properties similar to yours in our local Multiple Listing Service® (MLS®), and you are never under any obligation to buy or sell real estate through me. Best of all, it's FREE!

Again, "thanks" for being so kind and generous during our phone call, and please let me know if I can help in any way.

Sincerely,

[Agent Name]
[Agent Title]

Announcing New Neighbors

[Date]

«AddressBlock»

«GreetingLine»

Congratulations, you have new neighbors! I'm proud to announce the sale of *[Address of Property]* this week to *[Name of New Buyers]*. I hope you will give the *[Last Name of New Buyers]* a welcome to the neighborhood.

If you have real estate needs, feel free to call me, *[Agent's Name]*, at *[Phone Number]*. You can also visit my web site at *[Web Address]* to view properties for sale and find more real estate information.

Now is a great time to buy or sell a home! For a FREE price evaluation on what your home is worth on today's real estate market, call me at *[Phone Number]*.

Thanks for your time, and I hope you extend a hearty welcome to *[Name of New Buyers]*.

Sincerely,

[Agent Name]
[Agent Title]

Note: Please obtain buyer's permission prior to using this letter!

[Date]

«AddressBlock»

«GreetingLine»

I want you to know that I still want to help you market your property, if you are interested in doing so. I have enclosed some more information for you to look over. Please give me a call if you need further explanation on this information.

You have a lovely house, and I enjoyed our visit when I was out there. As I mentioned before, "thank you" for allowing me the opportunity to meet with you about your real estate needs. Please let me know if I can help.

Sincerely,

[Agent Name]
[Agent Title]

Sphere of Influence

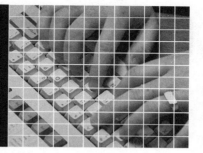

According to the *2003 National Association of REALTORS® Profile of Homebuyers and Sellers*, nearly one-half of all buyers indicated they found their real estate agents by a referral from a friend, family member, or neighbor. Do you realize the power and importance of that statistic? Most buyers used a particular real estate agent because someone recommended that agent!

If you're not using a method to correspond with your sphere of influence regularly, then please do so, starting today. Included in this section are various sphere of influence letters for you to use. Of course, the true power of using your sphere of influence should be a combination of personal contacts, such as phone calls, birthday cards, and short notes. With this approach and the letters in this book, you can now correspond with your sphere of influence for months to come.

Introductory Letter—Sphere of Influence

[Date]

«AddressBlock»

«GreetingLine»

I am excited to announce my affiliation with *[Agency Name]* in *[City]*, *[State]*. After successfully completing my educational requirements and passing the state real estate exam, I am now ready to serve you with your real estate needs. *[Agency Name]* offers a continuous and detailed training program for their new agents to assure their clients and customers the same quality service others have come to expect.

I want you to be aware of a couple of key points about the real estate industry:

- According to a recent survey by The National Association of REALTORS®, most buyers found their real estate agents by recommendations from a family member, neighbor, or friend.
- The real estate industry normally pays agents on commission sales. In other words, I am paid only if I am involved in a real estate transaction with a buyer or seller.
- Referrals from you are a key ingredient to the growth of my business!

I hope you will think of me if you know of someone interested in buying or selling real estate. Please give that person my name and phone number, or feel free to call me with the name and phone number so I can make the first contact. Your help will play an integral role in my development as a real estate professional!

Thank you for your help, *[Letter Name]*, and I appreciate your friendship and support.

Sincerely,

[Agent Name]
[Agent Title]

Accepting New Clients

[Date]

«AddressBlock»

«GreetingLine»

The busy buying-and-selling real estate season is here, and I am now accepting new clients! That's right! If you know of someone in the market to buy or sell a home, I can help.

Now is a great time to buy or sell a home, and I am in a good position to devote my experience and time to new buyers and sellers. I would appreciate your recommendation to anyone you know interested in buying or selling a home. Thank you!

I hope all is well with you, [Client's Name], and I thank you for your time.

Sincerely,

[Agent Name]
[Agent Title]

[Date]

«AddressBlock»

«GreetingLine»

Hello! I hope all is well with you and your family. I wanted to write and tell you thanks again for your support and business. Thank you! Did you know that according to the *2003 National Association of REALTORS® Profile of Home Buyers and Sellers*, over one-half of all buyers found their real estate agents through recommendations from a friend, neighbor, or family member? That's right, over 50 percent of all homebuyers find their agents by referrals from someone. Because this is such a big concern for homebuyers today, I wanted to ask you to remember me when you hear of a friend or neighbor considering the services of a real estate professional. I would love to help your friends, and it would be an honor for me to work with them.

Again, thank you for your support and friendship, *[Client's Name]*, and think of me when you think of real estate.

Sincerely,

[Agent Name]
[Agent Title]

Wanted—Buyers and Sellers

[Date]

«AddressBlock»

«GreetingLine»

Wanted! Buyers and sellers, any price range, any location!

Sometimes I would like to be that blunt with my advertising, but I know it wouldn't be effective in my marketplace. One great reason I do not have to resort to that kind of advertising is because of a good referral base from my friends and family. Thank you!

Right now my inventory is low. Most of my current buyers have found homes to buy, and my current listings have sold. It's good news, but for a real estate professional like myself it also means my business will begin to slow down if I do not restore my inventory of buyers and sellers. If you know of someone in the market to buy or sell real estate, please let that person know about me.

I hope all is well with you and your family, and I appreciate your continued support with my real estate career. Thanks again for your referrals!

Sincerely,

[Agent Name]
[Agent Title]

Average Sales Price—Specific Area

[Date]

«AddressBlock»

«GreetingLine»

I thought you might like to know about the latest sales figures from [City] or [Neighborhood or Subdivision]. Below is a brief explanation for the average sales price, number of days a typical home is on the market from list date to sale date, and the percentage of list price to sales price.

Number Sold	Average Sales Price	Days on Market	% of List to Sales Price

My goal is to provide this information to you quarterly; however, feel free to contact me any time you would like to know this, and I will gladly provide it to you.

I appreciate your time and I hope you will think of me if you know of someone interested in buying or selling real estate. Please give that person my name and phone number or feel free to call me with the name and phone number so I can make the first contact. Your help will play an integral role in my development as a real estate professional!

Thank you for your support [Letter Name].

Sincerely,

[Agent Name]
[Agent Title]

Average Sales Price—Multiple Areas

[Date]

«AddressBlock»

«GreetingLine»

I thought you might like to know about the latest sales figures from [City] or [Neighborhood or Subdivision]. Below is a brief explanation for the average sales price, number of days a typical home is on the market from list date to sale date, and the percentage of list price to sales price.

City	Number Sold	Average Sales Price	Days on Market	% of List to Sales Price

My goal is to provide this information to you quarterly; however, feel free to contact me any time you would like to know this and I will gladly provide it to you.

I appreciate your time and I hope you will think of me if you know of someone interested in buying or selling real estate. Please give that person my name and phone number or feel free to call me with the name and phone number so I can make the first contact. Your help will play an integral role in my development as a real estate professional!

Thank you for your support, [Letter Name].

Sincerely,

[Agent Name]
[Agent Title]

Spring Letter

[Date]

«AddressBlock»

«GreetingLine»

It's great to see green grass and flowers in blossom, and to hear birds singing again, not to mention the increase in real estate bustle at our office. Spring is always an enjoyable time of the year for many people. I hope you're having a great month and enjoying this season change too!

I wanted to write and remind you of how my success in real estate is dependent on referrals from friends like you. Do you know of someone considering buying or selling? If so, please let that person know of my services. Many agents (including myself) appreciate and value the referrals sent to us from our friends and family members. Thank you for always promoting my name when you hear of someone thinking about buying or selling real estate.

I appreciate your time, *[Letter Name]*, and if you need help with any real estate needs yourself, remember I am only a phone call away.

Sincerely,

[Agent Name]
[Agent Title]

Summer Letter

[Date]

«AddressBlock»

«GreetingLine»

I hope you're having a great year! Summer is here, and the real estate market is still going strong. Don't forget, if you know of someone considering buying or selling, be sure to give that person my name. I love referrals, and these leads from friends like you are critical to my business success.

I appreciate your time, *[Letter Name]*, and if you need help with any real estate needs yourself, remember I am only a phone call away. I hope this year continues to bring much happiness to you and your family, and again, "thank you" for your support!

Sincerely,

[Agent Name]
[Agent Title]

Fall Letter

[Date]

«AddressBlock»

«GreetingLine»

The late author and journalist Jim Bishop once said, *"Autumn carries more gold in its hand than all the other seasons."* I hope you're having a great year, and I hope you're enjoying this wonderful change of season. Our real estate market is still strong, and I'm looking forward to a great third quarter in real estate sales.

Don't forget, if you know of someone considering buying or selling real estate, be sure to give that person my name. I love referrals, and these leads that friends like you provide are critical to my business success.

I appreciate your time, *[Letter Name]*, and don't forget, if you need help with any real estate needs, I'm only a phone call away.

As always, "thank you" for your support!

Sincerely,

[Agent Name]
[Agent Title]

Winter Letter

[Date]

«AddressBlock»

«GreetingLine»

Odd as it may seem, winter is often an excellent time to sell real estate! Why? Generally there is still a good supply of buyers looking for real estate but a smaller number of properties to choose from. These conditions make what we sometimes refer to as a "sellers market." Unfortunately, many sellers take their real estate off the market until springtime, thinking this is the best time to sell. True, spring is an excellent time to list real estate, but the competition is much greater, allowing buyers more to choose from.

If you know of someone considering a move soon, please remind that person of my services. The success of my career is dependent on referrals from friends like you, and despite what many people may claim, now is a great time to buy or sell real estate!

I appreciate your time, *[Letter Name]*, and thanks in advance for always remembering me when you think of real estate.

Sincerely,

[Agent Name]
[Agent Title]

Follow-Up Letter—Article Enclosed

[Date]

«AddressBlock»

«GreetingLine»

I hope all is going well with you. I read this article about real estate and wanted to share it with you.

Now is a great time to buy or sell real estate. I appreciate your friendship, *[Letter Name]*, and please keep me in mind if I can help you with your real estate needs.

Sincerely,

[Agent Name]
[Agent Title]

Letters to Buyers

There are usually three types of real estate buyers you will come into contact with as a real estate professional:

1. Cold
2. Medium
3. Hot

Cold buyers are those prospects who want to look at houses but are not ready to buy. They might have credit issues to correct, job promotions in the future, or many other reasons why their home purchases cannot take place. Many real estate trainers and coaches will tell you not to waste time working with these types of buyers. True, you don't need to run the wheels off your car showing to this category of buyers, but you do need to communicate with them so that when they become "hot" buyers you're the agent they think of! In this section you'll find a collection of letters to help you remain in contact with this group of prospects.

Medium buyers want to buy homes, but have no great need to buy right now unless the right home comes along. Again, communication is critical, as medium-type buyers will buy at some point in the future.

Hot buyers are the clients everyone is looking for, and few agents understand the key to retaining and keeping these types of buyers in their corner. Again, communication

becomes a priceless commodity to the hot buyers. Acknowledging your appreciation for working with them during the home-buying process, keeping them informed on what happens before and after the sale, and general follow-up about new listings and other information will help your business tenfold.

If you have not used some of the types of letters for buyers included in this section, I encourage you to begin doing so today.

Asking for Letter of Recommendation

[Date]

«AddressBlock»

«GreetingLine»

I hope you are enjoying your new home! As you know, much of my business comes from referrals from past clients such as you. I always count it an honor when someone refers a buyer or seller to me, and gives me a high recommendation. Thank you for being so kind as to mention my name when you hear of someone wanting to buy or sell real estate!

Sometimes in my business I deal with prospects whom I've never met, and they, unfortunately, do not know of anyone who has used my services. Although this is not a big obstacle for me to overcome, sometimes it is good to show testimonial letters from my previous clients to them. If you could write a short note recommending my services that I could use in my advertising and marketing programs, I would appreciate it.

As always, "thank you" for allowing me to be of service to you with your real estate needs.

Sincerely,

[Agent Name]
[Agent Title]

Asking for Referral

[Date]

«AddressBlock»

«GreetingLine»

I hope you have settled into your new home and everything is going well for you! I do appreciate your business, and I want you to know that you can count on me after the sale too. Please feel free to call me if you have a problem or a need arises in the future.

One of the key ingredients to making my business successful is referrals from past clients, like you, and people I know. If you know of someone in the market to buy or sell a home, please let that person know about me, and see if I can have permission to contact him or her. It would be a great compliment and honor to handle your friends' real estate needs.

Again, "thank you" for allowing me the privilege of helping you with your real estate needs. I appreciate your time.

Sincerely,

[Agent Name]
[Agent Title]

Asking for Testimonial Letter

[Date]

«AddressBlock»

«GreetingLine»

Can you believe three months have gone by since you bought your new home? Wow, time goes by quickly! I hope you have settled into your new home and everything is going well for you. I do appreciate your business, and I hope we can work together on another real estate transaction in the future.

Much of my business is from referrals from past clients, like you, and from friends and family members. Referrals are a major contributor to the success of my business. However, there are times when I work with out-of-town clients or people who just don't know me and might be deciding whether to choose me or someone else. For those instances, it is helpful for me to have testimonial letters to show these prospects how others have viewed my services. I thought of you, *[Client's Name]*, and wondered if you would send me a brief testimonial letter I could use in my marketing material. If this is something you might do for me, I would appreciate it. If you prefer not to do this, I understand.

Again, "thank you" for allowing me the opportunity to help you with your real estate needs. I hope you enjoy your new home and that you can call it home for many more years!

Sincerely,

[Agent Name]
[Agent Title]

Call—Buyers Relocating from Other Area

[Date]

«AddressBlock»

«GreetingLine»

"Thanks" for your phone call today about properties for sale in our area. I have enclosed a sample packet of information on the *[Name of Your Area]* area, as well as homes for sale matching the description you provided me. Please note that some of the listings enclosed in this packet are with other agents and agencies. However, I can still be your main point of contact for viewing any of these listings.

You can also preview any of our properties online at *[Your Web Site Address]*. Many of our properties on our web site have extra photos and virtual tours, which leads me to my next point, photos. Please feel free to let me know if there is a listing included that you have an interest in but would like to see more photographs of. If the seller and other agent give permission, I will be glad to take and provide more photos for you before your trip to our area. My goal is to provide you with as much useful information as possible before your arrival so you can make an informed decision on your next home purchase.

I look forward in meeting you and your family when you visit the area, and I hope the enclosed information is helpful. Again, "thank you" for allowing me to help you with your real estate needs during your move.

Yours truly,

[Agent Name]
[Agent Title]

Follow-Up with Cold Prospect #1

[Date]

«AddressBlock»

«GreetingLine»

I hope things are going well for you. I realize your home purchase is on hold for a while, but I thought you might like to keep informed on what is for sale in the local market. I've enclosed a group of new listings matching the information you provided me when we were looking for houses a while back. Again, I felt you might like to periodically review current homes and their prices.

Please keep me in mind when you are ready to buy your new home. I would love to help you. Thanks for your time.

Sincerely,

[Agent Name]
[Agent Title]

Follow-Up with Cold Prospect #2

[Date]

«AddressBlock»

«GreetingLine»

I know it's been a while since I last spoke with you about your real estate needs. I hope things are going well for you. I've enclosed a group of new listings matching the information you provided me when we were looking for houses a while back. I don't want to pressure you in any way, but I did want to keep you updated on the latest new listings for sale in our area. If you see a home in the enclosed information that you would like to look at, please let me know.

As always, keep me in mind when you are ready to buy your new home. I would love to help you. Thanks for your time.

Sincerely,

[Agent Name]
[Agent Title]

Follow-Up with Cold Prospect #3

[Date]

«AddressBlock»

«GreetingLine»

Hello, and how are you doing? I do not know if you're still interested in finding a new home, but I've enclosed a group of new listings matching the information you provided me when we were looking for houses a while back. I don't want to pressure you in any way, but I did want to keep you updated on the latest new listings for sale in our area. If you see a home in the enclosed information that you would like to look at, please let me know.

As always, keep me in mind when you are ready to buy your new home. I would love to help you. Thanks for your time, and I hope to hear from you soon.

Sincerely,

[Agent Name]
[Agent Title]

Follow-Up with Cold Prospect #4

[Date]

«AddressBlock»

«GreetingLine»

I hope all is going well with you. I was updating my records and came across your name and wondered how you were doing. If you have not purchased a home yet, it's still an excellent time to own your own home! I would love to visit with you about your present needs and wants for your future dream home. Feel free to call me any time you are ready to buy your new home.

I have enclosed a few listings for you to preview based on the information you had provided me before when we were looking at homes.

I hope to hear from you soon, and again I hope all is well with you.

Sincerely,

[Agent Name]
[Agent Title]

Follow-Up with Medium Prospect

[Date]

«AddressBlock»

«GreetingLine»

I hope things are going well for you. I've enclosed a group of new listings matching the information you provided me when we were looking for houses a while back. If you see a home in the enclosed information that you would like to look at, please let me know.

As always, keep me in mind when you are ready to buy your new home. I would love to help you. Thanks for your time, and I hope to hear from you soon.

Sincerely,

[Agent Name]
[Agent Title]

[Date]

«AddressBlock»

«GreetingLine»

It's been some time since we last visited about your possible home purchase, and I recognize your need to take a short break from the house-hunting market. However, I just noticed a new listing that meets the features you wanted, and want to share it with you. I hope the enclosed flyer answers all of your questions. Please let me know if you would like to arrange an appointment to preview this listing.

As always, "thank you" for allowing me the opportunity to be of service to you with your real estate needs. Let me know when you are ready to begin looking at homes again.

Sincerely,

[Agent Name]
[Agent Title]

Invitation to Buyers' Seminar— Cold Prospect

[Date]

«AddressBlock»

«GreetingLine»

Hello, and how are you doing? I know we have not spoken for some time about your home-buying decision. If you are still in the market for a home, I would love to invite you to a FREE homebuyers' seminar on *[Date and Time]*, at *[Location]*. This special evening will help you learn more about:

- ✓ How to buy a home with NO money down!
- ✓ How to avoid the ten common mistakes most homebuyers make!
- ✓ How to avoid paying too much in closing costs and other "junk lender fees!"
- ✓ How you can have "buyer's representation" during the home-buying process!
- ✓ Why getting a home inspection is important!
- ✓ Insurance tips and money-saving ideas to protect your investment!
- ✓ And much more!

If you're interested in attending the seminar, please RSVP to *[Phone Number]* by *[Date]*. Although I recommend reservations because of seating limits, please feel free to stop by if you are unable to call in advance. And yes, it's fine to bring a friend!

Owning your own home is one of the greatest pleasures in life, not to mention the financial benefits associated with homeownership. Now is a great time to buy your own home! Come find out all the answers to your questions this *[Date, Time]* at *[Location]*.

I appreciate your allowing me to work with you in the past for your real estate needs, and please call me any time you need help in the future. I hope you can attend our homebuyers' seminar.

Sincerely,

[Agent Name]
[Agent Title]

Invitation to Buyers' Seminar— General Letter

[Date]

«AddressBlock»

«GreetingLine»

You're invited to a FREE homebuyers' seminar on *[Date and Time]*, at *[Location]*. This special evening will help you learn more about:

- ✓ How to buy a home with NO money down!
- ✓ How to avoid the ten common mistakes most homebuyers make!
- ✓ How to avoid paying too much in closing costs and other "junk lender fees!"
- ✓ How you can have "buyer's representation" during the home-buying process!
- ✓ Why getting a home inspection is important!
- ✓ Insurance tips and money-saving ideas to protect your investment!
- ✓ And much more!

To accept this special invitation to our homebuyers' seminar, please RSVP to *[Phone Number]* by *[Date]*. Although we recommend reservations because of seating limits, please feel free to stop by if you are unable to call in advance. And yes, it's fine to bring a friend!

Owning your own home is one of the greatest pleasures in your life, not to mention the financial benefits associated with homeownership. Now is a great time to buy your own home! Come find out all the answers to your questions this *[Date, Time]* at *[Location]*.

Don't forget, it's FREE! Call *[Phone Number]* to reserve your seat today!

Sincerely,

[Agent Name]
[Agent Title]

Buyer Possibly Relocating to Area

[Date]

«AddressBlock»

«GreetingLine»

I received your letter today about your need for information about our area. First, "thank you" for your inquiry and the opportunity to help you! I have enclosed a sample packet of information on the *[Name of Your Area]* area, as well as homes for sale matching the description you provided me. Please note that some of the listings enclosed in this packet are with other agents and agencies; however, I can still be your main point of contact for viewing any of these listings.

You can also preview any of our properties online at *[Your Web Site Address]*. Many of the properties on our web site have extra photos and virtual tours, which leads me to my next point, photos. Please feel free to let me know if there is a listing included that you have an interest in but would like to see more photographs of. If the seller and other agent give permission, I will be glad to take and provide more photos for you before your trip to our area. My goal is to provide you with as much useful information as possible before your arrival so you can make an informed decision on your next home purchase.

I look forward to meeting you and your family should you make a visit to our area, and hope the enclosed information is helpful. Again, "thank you" for your letter, and I hope to hear from you soon.

Yours truly,

[Agent Name]
[Agent Title]

Providing Information to Buyers about Area

[Date]

«AddressBlock»

«GreetingLine»

It was nice to speak with you on the telephone today, and, as you requested, I have enclosed information about our local area and schools. I have also enclosed information on available real estate for sale in our area for you to review. Please call me with any more questions you might have about our area.

Keep in mind that you can also find out more information about homes for sale at my web site at *[Web Site Address]*.

I appreciate your allowing me the opportunity to provide this information to you, and that you find it helpful. I hope to hear from you soon.

Sincerely,

[Agent Name]
[Agent Title]

Informing Buyer of Price Reduction

[Date]

«AddressBlock»

«GreetingLine»

I hope things are going well for you! I wanted to let you know the property I showed you at [Address of Property] has a new reduced price. The new price is now [New Price]. If you still have an interest in this property, please let me know. If you would like to preview the property again, it is no problem for me to arrange an appointment. I have enclosed another flyer for you to read more about it.

As always, *"thank you"* for allowing me the opportunity to be of service to you with your real estate needs, and I hope to hear from you soon.

Sincerely,

[Agent Name]
[Agent Title]

Thank You for Attending Open House

[Date]

«AddressBlock»

«GreetingLine»

I wanted to say *"thank you"* for taking time out of your busy schedule to visit my open house this past weekend at *[Address of Open House]*. I hope you enjoyed the tour and hope the additional information about the house was sufficient for you. If you would like to view more information about this home, please check out my web site at *[Your Web Address]*.

Would you like to be the first to learn of new listings in your area? If so, please call or write me at *[Your Phone Number and E-Mail Address]* and provide me with a brief description of what you are looking for. I can set up a saved search in our Multiple Listing Service® to notify both you and me of new listings the instant they're placed on the market. There's no cost or obligation for me to do this for you, and, best of all, we'll both have firsthand knowledge of those great buys that become available before anyone else.

Again, *[Letter Name]*, *"thank you"* for visiting my open house, and please let me know if I can help you in any way with your real estate needs.

Yours truly,

[Agent Name]
[Agent Title]

Thank You for Calling Office— Multiple Homes

[Date]

«AddressBlock»

«GreetingLine»

Thank you for calling my real estate office today about real estate for sale in our area. Enclosed you will find properties currently on the real estate market in the price range you suggested. Please keep in mind that I can help you with any properties you might find through the newspaper, Internet, by driving around, or through an open house, regardless of whom they are listed with. I will continue to check our Multiple Listing Service® for any new listings that might be of interest to you. I hope this information is helpful.

Again, *"thank you"* for calling my office.

Sincerely,

[Agent Name]
[Agent Title]

Thank You for Stopping by Office

[Date]

«AddressBlock»

«GreetingLine»

I appreciate your stopping by our office today and your interest in buying real estate. I hope the information I provided you was helpful. Please keep in mind that I can help you with any properties you might find through the newspaper, Internet, by driving around, or through an open house, regardless of whom they are listed with. I will continue to check our Multiple Listing Service® for any new listings that might be of interest to you.

Again, *"thank you"* for stopping by my office.

Sincerely,

[Agent Name]
[Agent Title]

Thank You—Working as Buyer's Agent

[Date]

«AddressBlock»

«GreetingLine»

I wanted to write you a short letter and tell you "thanks" for allowing me the opportunity to work with you as your buyer's representative. I have created a saved search in our Multiple Listing Service® (MLS®) matching the information you provided me for the type of property you want. Should any new listings become available in our MLS®, the computer will notify me by e-mail, and I can then contact you about the new listing.

Please let me know if you find any properties through the newspaper, by driving around, at open houses, etc. As your buyer's representative, it is important that you contact me first. I can then get the information for you and arrange any showings. If you do visit an open house be sure to explain to the agent on duty that you are working with me and that I am representing you as your buyer's agent. Trust me, the representative on duty at the open house will appreciate knowing this in advance!

As always, *"thank you"* for allowing me the opportunity to be of service to you with your real estate needs, and I feel certain we will find the property you are looking for soon.

Sincerely,

[Agent Name]
[Agent Title]

Showing Buyer—Single Home

[Date]

«AddressBlock»

«GreetingLine»

Just a quick note to say *"thank you"* for allowing me the opportunity to show you *[Address of Property Shown]* on *[Date of Showing]* of this week. Please let me know if there is any extra information I can get for you about this listing.

I will continue to check new properties for sale and let you know if anything looks as though it would be of interest to you. Again, thanks, and I will be in touch with you soon.

Sincerely,

[Agent Name]
[Agent Title]

[Date]

«AddressBlock»

«GreetingLine»

Just a quick note to say *"thank you"* for allowing me the opportunity to show you homes for sale in our area this week. Please let me know if there is any more information I can get for you on any of these listings.

I will continue to check new properties for sale and let you know if anything looks as though it would be of interest to you. Again, thanks, and I will be in touch with you soon.

Sincerely,

[Agent Name]
[Agent Title]

Important Dates after Contract Acceptance

[Date]

«AddressBlock»

«GreetingLine»

Just a reminder about the important dates we discussed concerning your contract on *[Property Address]*. I have listed below our duties and the dates by which these procedures must be completed:

☐	All inspections completed	*[Date]*
☐	Financing Approval	*[Date]*
☐	Other contingencies *[List]*	*[Date]*
☐	Closing	*[Date]*

It is critical that we meet all of these dates on time so you will stay on track with your sales contract with your contingencies. If not, I will need to ask for an extension to your contract on the issues you feel you cannot comply with. Please note that it is better for us to try to fulfill the dates listed above before the time frame if possible. This will allow us plenty of time to respond to any problems that might arise.

As always, "thank you" for allowing me the opportunity to be of service to you with your real estate needs. Please call me if you have any questions. I'll be in touch.

Yours truly,

[Agent Name]
[Agent Title]

Pre-Closing Letter

[Date]

«AddressBlock»

«GreetingLine»

A reminder that our closing date is *[Date for Closing]*, at *[Escrow Agency Location]*, in *[City]* at *[Closing Time]*. We will perform our final walk-through before the closing at *[Time for Final Walk-Through]*. I have enclosed a checklist for you to review before the closing date.

As always, I appreciate your business and please let me know if there is anything I can do between now and the closing.

Sincerely,

[Agent Name]
[Agent Title]

Thank-You after the Sale

[Date]

«AddressBlock»

«GreetingLine»

Wow, it's finally finished! It seems like yesterday that we started our home search for you. I hope that you find your new home a delight to live in, and that you enjoy many wonderful memories there. I enjoyed our time together so much, and feel as though I have made new friends. Again, thank you!

Please keep my name and business card available for anyone you know looking to buy or sell real estate. As you know, my business is dependent on referrals from friends like you. I have enclosed several business cards for you to give out should you know of someone interested in buying or selling real estate.

Again, "thank you" for your business, and please know that I am here long after the sale for any needs you might have or help you might need. Enjoy your new home!

Sincerely,

[Agent Name]
[Agent Title]

Thank-You after Sale When Problems Arose

[Date]

«AddressBlock»

«GreetingLine»

Well, it's finally over! I did want to write and apologize for the mix-up at the closing this week. Unfortunately, sometimes a last-minute curveball is thrown at us. I appreciate your understanding during this problem and for being so considerate.

As always, "thank you" for your business, and please let me know if I can help in the future.

Sincerely,

[Agent Name]
[Agent Title]

Return of Earnest Money

[Date]

«AddressBlock»

«GreetingLine»

Enclosed you will find an earnest money check for *[Amount of Money]*, *[Check #]* for the deposit you had placed on property in *[City Location]*.

I am sorry things did not work out for you on this transaction, but please feel free to call me if you decide to look for other properties in our area.

Thank you for allowing *[Agency Name]* the opportunity to be of service to you with your real estate needs.

Sincerely,

[Agent Name]
[Agent Title]

[Date]

«AddressBlock»

«GreetingLine»

I wanted to write you a short letter and tell you "thanks" for allowing me the opportunity to work with you on finding a home in our community. I am sorry that your offer did not work out for the home at *[Address of Home Where Offer Was Made]*. I know you're disappointed that your search in our area did not provide you with anything, and I understand your need to look elsewhere for a home. I wish you the best of luck looking for a home in *[Address of City]*, and if you decide to look in our area again please give me a call. I would love to help you find your new home.

As always, *"thank you"* for allowing me the opportunity to be of service to you with your real estate needs, and, again, good luck in finding your new home.

Sincerely,

[Agent Name]
[Agent Title]

Thank You When Buyer Bought Elsewhere

[Date]

«AddressBlock»

«GreetingLine»

It was nice to speak with you on the telephone today and I am glad you found a piece of property that met your needs. I appreciated the opportunity you provided me to help you with your new home search, and I wish my efforts would have been more fruitful. Nevertheless, I am excited for you and wish you well with your new purchase.

Please keep me in mind if I can ever help you with your real estate needs in the future. Again, "thank you" and good luck!

Sincerely,

[Agent Name]
[Agent Title]

Tax Bill Letter

[Date]

«AddressBlock»

«GreetingLine»

Enclosed is the tax bill for the property you bought through *[Agency Name]*. On the settlement statement at closing, the seller paid *[His, Her]* portion of the taxes and you had a credit with taxes from January 1 through the day of closing. Therefore, you will need to pay these taxes before *[Tax Deadline Date]* to avoid any penalties. I know sometimes this seems a bit confusing, so please feel free to call me if you have any questions.

As always, *"thank you"* for allowing me the opportunity to be of service to you with your real estate needs.

Sincerely,

[Agent Name]
[Agent Title]

Letters to Sellers

What's the number-one complaint heard from most sellers of real estate today who are under a listing contract with a real estate agent? "We never hear from our agent!" If you want to develop a long and successful tenure in the real estate business, communicate with your clients, especially sellers! Even if your phone call or letter is to say "I'm sorry, but we do not have anyone interested in your property now," communicate those words to them. Sellers want to know what's going on, even if that means nothing is happening.

This section includes an exhaustive list of letters you can use with your clients, from follow-up letters to thank-you letters to price reduction notes. This section will cover all of your letter needs for your sellers and allow you to communicate with them on a regular basis.

Don't forget the power and importance of a personal phone call or visit! However, communicating by mail is just one more way to keep your sellers happy with your service and recommending you to others for their real estate needs.

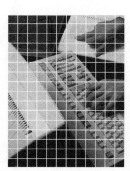

Request for Additional Information

[Date]

«AddressBlock»

«GreetingLine»

In preparing my listing packet for potential buyers, I realized the "additional information" form you had agreed to send me was not on file. Would you mind completing a brief description next to the questions I have included on the "Sellers Additional Information" form? This information will help me market your property to potential buyers. I have enclosed a self-addressed stamped envelope for you.

As always, "*thank you*" for allowing me the opportunity to be of service to you with your real estate needs, and please feel free to call me if you ever have any questions.

Sincerely,

[Agent Name]
[Agent Title]

Follow-Up after Agent Tour

[Date]

«AddressBlock»

«GreetingLine»

Just a note to tell you *"thanks"* for allowing our office to tour your real estate listing this week. Each week our office will tour the new listings to help our agents become more familiar with our inventory for property calls. We also ask the agents to fill out evaluation sheets with their thoughts are on price, marketability features, and anything we might do to improve the salability of your property. I will call you this week to go over those evaluation sheets.

I do appreciate your business and I hope that a SOLD sign will be here soon! Please feel free to call me if you have any questions, and again *"thank you"* for your business.

Yours truly,

[Agent Name]
[Agent Title]

Marketing Update

[Date]

«AddressBlock»

«GreetingLine»

I want to provide you with a quick update on where our marketing efforts are at this stage in our listing process, and I have enclosed my marketing update form that outlines my activities. If there is something you would like me to do that is not listed on the update form, please let me know and I will follow up with your suggestion.

As always, "*thank you*" for allowing me the opportunity to be of service to you with your real estate needs, and I will be in touch with you to keep you updated on the marketing activities for your home.

Sincerely,

[Agent Name]
[Agent Title]

Asking for Testimonial Letter

[Date]

«AddressBlock»

«GreetingLine»

Can you believe three months have gone by since I sold your house? Wow, time goes by quickly. I hope you have settled into your new home and all is well for you! I do appreciate your business, and I hope we can work together on another real estate transaction in the future.

Much of my business is from referrals from past clients like you, as well as friends and family members. Referrals are a major contributor to the success of my business. However, there are times when I work with out-of-town clients or people who just don't know me. For those instances, it is helpful for me to have testimonial letters to show these prospects how others have viewed my services. I thought of you, *[Letter Name]*, and wondered if you would send me a brief testimonial letter I could use in my marketing material. If this is something you could do for me, I would appreciate it. If you prefer not to, I understand.

Again, *"thank you"* for allowing me the opportunity to help you with your real estate needs.

Yours truly,

[Agent Name]
[Agent Title]

Asking for Letter of Recommendation

[Date]

«AddressBlock»

«GreetingLine»

I hope you're enjoying your new home! I wanted to write you a quick note to ask a favor of you. As you know, referrals from past clients and customers play a large part in the success of my business. Many times my new prospects would like to know a little bit more about me, and/or hear from other satisfied clients and customers. I was hoping you would be kind enough to write a short letter of recommendation for me that I could include with my listing presentations. This information would be priceless for me to include when I am visiting with customers who do not know me. Just a short note promoting me as your real estate agent would be helpful.

I would also like to remind you to remember me if you know of someone in the market wishing to buy or sell real estate. Because my business relies solely on commission, referrals from satisfied clients and customers mean a lot to me. If you would prefer to call me with any potential prospects, please feel free to do so any time. You can also e-mail me at [E-Mail Address].

Again, *thanks* for letting me serve you with your real estate needs. It was a real joy and a pleasure to work with you.

Yours truly,

[Agent Name]
[Agent Title]

General Follow-Up Letter

[Date]

«AddressBlock»

«GreetingLine»

Marketing real estate can be a rewarding and challenging experience. I know the first couple of weeks are exciting and stressful to many of my sellers. Making sure the house is in tip-top shape every day can become a burden, especially when you go to such lengths to do so and several days go by without anyone looking at your property. Unfortunately, that is the downside of marketing real estate. Don't give up, and always be ready to show your house, as today could be the day that someone wants to look at your house on a short notice.

Keep in mind that just because no one shows your property does not mean we have not had calls or inquiries. Our job is to screen all prospects to make sure they can financially afford a property like yours. We also make sure that everyone looking is serious about buying a home and not just out for a "pleasure" ride to preview houses.

Stay encouraged and think positive, and I feel certain we will have an interested prospect soon.

If at any time you would like to visit with me about some of the other marketing efforts for your property, or to think through some new marketing ideas, please give me a call.

As always, *"thank you"* for allowing me the opportunity to be of service to you with your real estate needs.

Sincerely,

[Agent Name]
[Agent Title]

Market Conditions Update—Letter #1

[Date]

«AddressBlock»

«GreetingLine»

It's time for my "General Market Condition Update." I have enclosed a form with this letter to show what is happening in our marketplace. I have made some notes on the information that is relevant and applies to our situation. I have also enclosed my marketing recap form since you first listed your property with me, which details the marketing activities I have set into place so far.

If at anytime you would like to visit with me about some of the other marketing efforts for your property, please give me a call. I am always open to new ideas and suggestions that you may have.

As always, "*thank you*" for allowing me the opportunity to be of service to you with your real estate needs, and if we both think positive I know a SOLD sign will be here soon!

Sincerely,

[Agent Name]
[Agent Title]

Market Conditions Update—Letter #2

[Date]

«AddressBlock»

«GreetingLine»

Here is another "General Market Condition Update." As with my previous updates, this form will help show what is happening in our marketplace. I have made some notes about the information that is relevant and applies to our situation. I have also enclosed my marketing recap form since you first listed your property with me, which details the marketing activities I have set into place so far.

If at any time you would like to visit me about some of the other marketing efforts for your property, please give me a call. I am always open to new ideas and suggestions that you may have.

As always, *"thank you"* for allowing me the opportunity to be of service to you with your real estate needs, and if we both think positive I know a SOLD sign will be here soon!

Sincerely,

[Agent Name]
[Agent Title]

Follow-Up with Business Cards

[Date]

«AddressBlock»

«GreetingLine»

Enclosed you will find some small business cards with your property photo and a brief description about your real estate for sale. As with any marketing plan, the key to a successful sale is to create as much interest as possible. This marketing idea is one good way to carry out that goal. Many of my clients like to have these cards to give out to friends and co-workers. It's a great way to help spread the word about your house, and might even lead to a potential buyer. Let me know if you need a few more cards, and I will be glad to print out another sheet for you.

As always, "*thank you*" for allowing me the opportunity to be of service to you with your real estate needs, and if we both think positive I know a SOLD sign will be here soon!

Sincerely,

[Agent Name]
[Agent Title]

Note: A template for the business cards is available on the CD-ROM.

Follow-Up with Flyers

[Date]

«AddressBlock»

«GreetingLine»

Enclosed you will find more flyers with your property photo and a brief description of your real estate for sale. If you could replace these flyers when our flyer box is empty, I would appreciate it. Let me know when you need more flyers, and I will have more prepared. If there is a feature you would like me to highlight on the property flyer, please let me know, and I will have it added immediately.

As always, "*thank you*" for allowing me the opportunity to be of service to you with your real estate needs, and if we both think positive I know a SOLD sign will be here soon!

Sincerely,

[Agent Name]
[Agent Title]

Marketing Flyer Enclosure

[Date]

«AddressBlock»

«GreetingLine»

I have enclosed a sample flyer I plan to send out to other agents and agencies in our area. Please let me know if you see something you would like changed or added to the flyer. My goal is to have these flyers mailed by the end of the week.

I appreciate your business, and as always, *"thank you"* for allowing me the opportunity to be of service to you with your real estate needs.

Sincerely,

[Agent Name]
[Agent Title]

Home Warranty Idea

[Date]

«AddressBlock»

«GreetingLine»

I realize your house has now been for sale for a while. I'm also sure you have legitimate concerns about why it hasn't sold. Unfortunately, several factors can contribute to this situation. Normally, the most important issue is price, and adjusting the price will always help. Another issue that plays a major role is the type of marketing features associated with the property. In other words, can we offer something of "value" to the prospective buyers so that they will choose our house over one offered by the competition? One idea is to offer a home warranty program to the new buyers. This is an excellent feature that covers many problems that can occur after the closing. This warranty gives the buyers peace of mind that if something does break down or go wrong, they may have insurance to cover it. I have enclosed information about home warranties for you. Please review this and decide if this is a marketing benefit you might want to offer. Keep in mind that there is no obligation to do this, it's just a suggestion to help with marketing your real estate.

I do appreciate the opportunity to be of service to you with your real estate needs, and don't hesitate to call me if you have any more questions about this home warranty program.

Sincerely,

[Agent Name]
[Agent Title]

New Listing in Neighborhood—Letter #1

[Date]

«AddressBlock»

«GreetingLine»

By now you know that I have listed *[Listing Client's Name]* home. I wanted to write you personally about their property and enclose a property data sheet for you. If you know of someone interested in *[Listing Client's Name]* home, please let me know, and I can arrange a private showing for him or her.

Are you thinking about selling your house? If so, I would love to provide you a FREE price evaluation on what your property is worth on today's real estate market. Call me as soon as possible so we can arrange a time that is good for you.

Thank you for passing along the enclosed flyer, and let me know if I can be of help with your real estate needs.

Sincerely,

[Agent Name]
[Agent Title]

[Date]

«AddressBlock»

«GreetingLine»

[Listing Client's Name] listed their house with me this past week. I wanted to write you personally about their property and enclose a property data sheet. Do you know someone interested in this property? If so, could you please let me know or pass along this flyer to that person? I would be happy to arrange a private showing for him or her to see this new listing.

Are you thinking about selling your house? If so, I would love to provide you a FREE price evaluation on what your property is worth on today's real estate market. Call me as soon as possible so we can arrange a time that is good for you.

Thank you for passing along the enclosed flyer, and let me know if I can be of help with your real estate needs.

Sincerely,

[Agent Name]
[Agent Title]

New Marketing Strategy—Letter #1

[Date]

«AddressBlock»

«GreetingLine»

I wanted to write and explain a new marketing strategy I have for your real estate currently listed with me. I know that your listing is going into its *[Current Days on Market]* of the marketing campaign. There is no need to panic at this point, and I hope the new marketing ideas I have will stimulate more interest in your property. Today, the average time on market for a home in *[City]* is *[Days on Market in Area]*. As I have noted before, many properties sell much sooner than the average days on market and some properties take a bit longer.

I have enclosed my marketing recap form since you first listed your property with me, which details the marketing activities I have set into place so far. I have also enclosed a "New Marketing Strategy" form outlining some of the new ideas I plan to complete over the next few weeks.

If at any time you would like to visit with me about some of the other marketing efforts of your property, please give me a call. I am always open to new ideas and suggestions that you have.

As always, "*thank you*" for allowing me the opportunity to be of service to you with your real estate needs, and if we both think positive I know a SOLD sign will be here soon!

Sincerely,

[Agent Name]
[Agent Title]

Price Adjustment Request—Letter #1

[Date]

«AddressBlock»

«GreetingLine»

I have some information I wanted to pass along to you. Based on my research of recently sold properties in your area, I feel our price is only helping our competition. What does this mean? Frankly, many of the buyers who have recently looked at your home did not buy yours because other homes for sale had something else that appealed to them better. I know that your property has as much to offer as the competition, but, as the report points out, most homes are selling for less than our listed price.

One good way to fix this problem is to adjust our price to just below or at the competition's pricing strategy. I would suggest that we adjust the price to *[New Price Recommendation]*. I know this will help us in marketing your property and I feel certain this will also jump-start our activity again on new showings. If you are interested in doing this, please sign the enclosed price adjustment form and return it to me in the enclosed envelope as soon as possible. I will make all the necessary changes and notify the agents in our area as soon as I receive this form back from you.

As always, "*thank you*" for allowing me the opportunity to be of service to you with your real estate needs, and if we both think positive I know a SOLD sign will be here soon!

Sincerely,

[Agent Name]
[Agent Title]

Price Adjustment Request—Letter #2

[Date]

«AddressBlock»

«GreetingLine»

I realize you wanted to wait on adjusting the price I had recommended before, but I felt it was in our best interest to revisit this pricing strategy again. As with most products in our economy, supply and demand play a major role in the price of the product. The more demand for a good or service, the higher the price. Also true about price is that when there are many goods and services offered for sale, and the demand is not present, prices fall. Unfortunately, we fall into the second scenario. The number of homes for sale is rather large, and we have a smaller number of buyers to choose from.

The good news is we can correct this problem. Based on my research (please note the enclosed sales report I have put together), I believe if we would adjust the price to *[New Price Recommendation]* our chances of finding a buyer will increase. I also feel certain this will help jump-start our activity again on new showings. If this is acceptable to you, please sign the enclosed price adjustment form and return it to me in the enclosed envelope as soon as possible. I will make all the necessary changes and notify the agents in our area as soon as I receive this form back from you.

As always, *"thank you"* for allowing me the opportunity to be of service to you with your real estate needs, and if we both think positive I know a SOLD sign will be here soon!

Sincerely,

[Agent Name]
[Agent Title]

Price Adjustment Request—Letter #3

[Date]

«AddressBlock»

«GreetingLine»

It is now *[Current Days on Market]* since you first listed your real estate with me. I sincerely appreciate your business and I do want you to know that *[Agency Name]* is doing everything possible to speed up a sale on your property. However, sometimes we have no control as to what happens with various properties. I hate to sound like a broken record, but unless we adjust the price to be more competitive with the other properties for sale in our area, our chances of selling will continue to decline. When buyers look at our property and then compare it to what else is for sale and the price range of our competition, we're passed over for a less expensive property. In other words, the consumer will substitute the least expensive product if all other items are similar. Based on my research (please note the enclosed sales report I have put together), I believe if we would adjust the price to *[New Price Recommendation]*, we can close that gap between our property and the least expensive properties. I also feel certain this will help jump-start our activity again on new showings. If this is acceptable to you, please sign the enclosed price adjustment form and return it to me in the enclosed envelope as soon as possible. I will make all the necessary changes and notify the agents in our area as soon as I receive this form back from you.

As always, "*thank you*" for allowing me the opportunity to be of service to you with your real estate needs, and if we both think positive I know a SOLD sign will be here soon!

Sincerely,

[Agent Name]
[Agent Title]

Thank You for Adjusting Price

[Date]

«AddressBlock»

«GreetingLine»

I wanted to say "*thank you*" for agreeing to adjust your price on the property I have listed. I believe this price drop will have a positive impact on my marketing efforts. I'll keep you posted on the feedback I receive from agents and potential clients about our new price.

As always, "*thank you*" for allowing me the opportunity to serve you with your real estate needs, and please don't hesitate to call me if you have any questions.

Yours truly,

[Agent Name]
[Agent Title]

Request to Place Yard Sign on Property

[Date]

«AddressBlock»

«GreetingLine»

Many of the agents in my office and the local area have asked me why your property does not have a sign in the yard. I explained to them that during our first listing interview you had requested that I not put a sign in the front yard. Unfortunately, this has become a big hindrance in my efforts to sell your property. Many homes sell as a result of consumers seeing yard signs in front of houses. Your property has such good curb appeal that without a sign we are limiting many good prospects. I wanted to write you a short note and ask you to reconsider the idea of allowing me to place a sign in your yard. This would be a boost to our marketing campaign and open a new avenue of buyers for us. I will call you in the next couple of days to discuss this with you in more detail. Please keep in mind that I can add a sign rider with the words "appointment only" if this would make you feel more comfortable about the sign placement.

As always, *"thank you"* for allowing me the opportunity to be of service to you with your real estate needs. Please feel free to call me if you ever have any questions, and I hope you will consider the strategy of using a for-sale sign.

Sincerely,

[Agent Name]
[Agent Title]

Request to Put Listing Information in MLS®

[Date]

«AddressBlock»

«GreetingLine»

Many of the agents in my office and the local area have asked me why your property is not in our local Multiple Listing Service® (MLS®). I explained to them that during our first listing interview you had requested it not be placed in the local MLS®. Unfortunately, this has become a big hindrance in my efforts to sell your property. Many homes are sold by other real estate agents, and by not including your listing in our MLS®, we miss many good potential buyers, as they or their agents do not know about your property for sale. I wanted to write you a short note and ask you to reconsider the idea of allowing me to market your property through our MLS®. This would be a boost to our marketing campaign and open a new avenue of buyers for us. I will call you in the next couple of days to discuss this with you in more detail.

As always, *"thank you"* for allowing me the opportunity to be of service to you with your real estate needs. Please feel free to call me if you ever have any questions, and I hope you will consider the strategy of using the MLS® in our marketing efforts.

Sincerely,

[Agent Name]
[Agent Title]

Listing on Market for One Week

[Date]

«AddressBlock»

«GreetingLine»

Well, it's our first week of marketing your real estate, and I wanted to update you on what has occurred and will occur early on during this listing period. I have detailed just a few marketing endeavors below:

- Property information placed in our local Multiple Listing Service® (MLS®).
- Property information sent to *[Web Address]*, as well as other web sites that *[Agency Name]* uses.
- Digital photos taken and uploaded to the proper web sites and MLS®.
- Letters and/or e-mails sent to top agents in our area announcing your property for-sale.
- Open house scheduled for *[Date of Open House]*.
- Agent tour completed, evaluation update to follow.
- Flyers prepared for distribution to potential customers.
- *[List Other Items Completed Here]*.

Naturally, there are many behind-the-scenes activities done daily to market and sell your property. I believe it is good to keep you in the loop on what we are doing to find a buyer, and let you know how busy the first couple of weeks can be during our initial listing period. So, if I haven't called this last week, please don't think I have forgotten about you.

If at any time you would like to visit with me about some of the other marketing efforts for your property, please give me a call. As always, *"thank you"* for allowing me the opportunity to be of service to you with your real estate needs.

Sincerely,

[Agent Name]
[Agent Title]

[Date]

«AddressBlock»

«GreetingLine»

I know that time goes by quickly, and yes, it doesn't seem possible, but approximately one month has passed since you listed your property with me. I know we have not had much activity on your house, but don't let this discourage you. Who knows, this might be our day or week to find that special buyer! The average time on market for a home in *[City]* is *[Days on Market in Area]*. Unfortunately, this is part of the real estate business that can be discouraging for a seller such as yourself; however, many properties sell much sooner than the average days on market as shown.

If at any time you would like to visit with me about some of the other marketing efforts for your property, please give me a call. I do plan to send a special reminder notice this week to some of the agents in our area promoting your property.

As always, "*thank you*" for allowing me the opportunity to be of service to you with your real estate needs, and if we both think positive I know a SOLD sign will be here soon!

Sincerely,

[Agent Name]
[Agent Title]

First Four Weeks—A Lot of Activity

[Date]

«AddressBlock»

«GreetingLine»

I know that time goes by quickly, and yes, it doesn't seem possible, but approximately one month has passed since you listed your property with me. I know we have had some lookers on your house, which is a positive note. If this trend continues (many lookers but no offers), then we might discuss our pricing strategy. Normally, when we have a lot of activity but no offers, it is an indication that buyers are purchasing other properties because of their value compared to this and other homes on the market. Don't get discouraged. This might be our day or week to find that special buyer. The average time on market for a home in [City] is [Days on Market in Area].

If at any time you would like to visit with me about some of the other marketing efforts for your property, please give me a call. I do plan to send a special reminder notice to some of the agents in our area promoting your property.

As always, "*thank you*" for allowing me the opportunity to be of service to you with your real estate needs, and if we both think positive I know a SOLD sign will be here soon!

Sincerely,

[Agent Name]
[Agent Title]

Eight Weeks—No Activity

[Date]

«AddressBlock»

«GreetingLine»

I know that as time goes by, it can be discouraging to wonder why your property has not sold. There are many answers to this question, and unfortunately trying to pinpoint the problem is not always easily done. According to my records, your property is now beginning its third month for sale on the market. Today, the average time on market for a home in [City] is [Days on Market]. Many properties sell much sooner than the average days on market as shown, and some properties take a bit longer. I have enclosed my marketing recap from since you first listed your property with me, which details the marketing I have set into place so far.

If at any time you would like to visit with me about some of the other marketing efforts for your property, please give me a call. I am always open to new ideas and suggestions that my clients come up with.

As always, "*thank you*" for allowing me the opportunity to be of service to you with your real estate needs, and if we both think positive I know a SOLD sign will be here soon!

Sincerely,

[Agent Name]
[Agent Title]

Twelve Weeks—No Activity

[Date]

«AddressBlock»

«GreetingLine»

It's now toward the end of our third month of the marketing process, and I wish I were writing you to explain the closing procedures for your upcoming sale. Don't panic; I feel certain that we will be there soon. As of today, the average time on market for a home in [City] is [Days on Market in Area]. Many properties sell much sooner than the average days on market as indicated, and some properties take a bit longer.

I have enclosed my marketing recap from since you first listed your property with me, which details the marketing activities I have set into place so far. If at any time you would like to visit with me about some of the other marketing efforts for your property, please give me a call. I am always open to new ideas and suggestions that you come up with.

As always, "*thank you*" for allowing me the opportunity to be of service to you with your real estate needs, and if we both think positive I know a SOLD sign will be here soon!

Sincerely,

[Agent Name]
[Agent Title]

Sixteen Weeks—No Activity

[Date]

«AddressBlock»

«GreetingLine»

It's now been approximately 112 days since you first listed your real estate with me. As I have mentioned before, I know that as time goes by it can become discouraging to wonder why your property has not sold. Again, there are many answers to this question, and, unfortunately, trying to pinpoint the problem is not always easily done.

Please know that I am doing everything possible to expedite a sale for you, and always feel free to share any ideas or suggestions you might have for marketing your property.

As always, "*thank you*" for allowing me the opportunity to be of service to you with your real estate needs.

Sincerely,

[Agent Name]
[Agent Title]

Promoting Web Site

[Date]

«AddressBlock»

«GreetingLine»

Enclosed you will find a copy of your listing from my Internet web site. Please keep in mind that we're limited in the information we can list about your property on the Internet. However, if there is something missing from the description I have listed, please call me so we can discuss its addition to the site.

This is just another way [Agent or Agency Name] markets your real estate to the public. With my own web site, your home has exposure 365 days a year, 24 hours a day! The Internet has now surpassed the newspaper as an informational source for buyers looking for the homes of their dreams. According to the *2003 National Association of REALTORS® Profile of Home Buyers and Sellers*, **65 percent of all buyers used the Internet as an information source in finding homes**. If you want to visit my web site and see your home, just go to [Web Site]. *(Add next sentence if applicable to you)* In addition, your listing is featured on http://www.realtor.com, which is one of the most visited web sites by buyers today.

These are just a few of my commitments in promoting your property to its fullest, in finding a buyer for you.

As always, "*thank you*" for allowing me the opportunity to be of service to you with your real estate needs. I do hope a SOLD sign will be here soon, and do call me if you have any questions.

Yours truly,

[Agent Name]
[Agent Title]

Where Buyers Come From

[Date]

«AddressBlock»

«GreetingLine»

As our marketing efforts for your real estate continue, I wanted to share with you a few pieces of information on where buyers normally find their homes. The following statistics are provided through the *2003 National Association of REALTORS® Profile of Home Buyers and Sellers Guide.*

- 86% used a real estate agent for information sources.
- 69% noticed the yard sign.
- 65% searched the Internet.

As noted above, many of our best leads will come from other real estate agents in our community, and through the local MLS®. Please rest assured that I am doing everything possible to keep your property in front of many other real estate agents in our area on a daily basis. This is a key element in getting your real estate sold, and one that I do not take lightly.

As always, *"thank you"* for allowing me the opportunity to be of service to you with your real estate needs, and if we both think positive I know a SOLD sign will be here soon!

Sincerely,

[Agent Name]
[Agent Title]

Thank You for Listing—Letter #1

[Date]

«AddressBlock»

«GreetingLine»

I would like to say *"thank you"* for allowing me to serve you in your real estate needs. I recognize the confidence and trust you have placed in my company and me, and I assure you that I will strive to give you the best service available!

From the information you provided, and my own inspection, I prepared a property fact sheet on your listing. This fact sheet will be available in my office for prospective buyers, and I will also use this information to send to other real estate agencies in our area. I am enclosing a copy for you to read over. Please let me know of any corrections or additions you would like for me to make.

I have provided information to our local Multiple Listing Service® (MLS®) organization, which will give hundreds of other real estate agents in our area access to your property. This enables not only [Agency Name] to try to find a buyer, but other companies as well. I do promise that I will do everything possible to qualify potential buyers before someone shows your property.

My goal is twofold:

- *To get your property sold in the fastest time frame possible, thereby earning you the maximum amounts of money for your investment.*
- *To make sure my service is satisfactory to you!*

Good communication between us means I can do a better job for you. Please feel free to call me any time if you have any questions or comments about the marketing efforts on your property.

As always, *"thank you"* for allowing me the opportunity to be of service to you with your real estate needs.

Sincerely,

[Agent Name]
[Agent Title]

Thank You for Listing—Letter #2

[Date]

«AddressBlock»

«GreetingLine»

I would like to say "*thank you*" for allowing me to serve you in your real estate needs. I recognize the confidence and trust you have placed in my company and me, and I assure you that I will strive to give you the best service available in our area!

From the information you have provided and my own inspection, I prepared a property fact sheet on your listing. This fact sheet will be available in my office for prospective buyers, and I will also use this information to send to other real estate agencies in our area. I am enclosing a copy for you to read over. Please feel free to let me know of any corrections or additions you would like me to make.

I have provided information to our local MLS® organization, which will give hundreds of other real estate agents in our area access to your property. This enables not only *[Agency Name]* to try to find a buyer, but other companies as well. I do promise that I will do everything possible to qualify potential buyers before someone shows your property.

As always, "*thank you*" for allowing me the opportunity to be of service to you with your real estate needs.

Sincerely,

[Agent Name]
[Agent Title]

Thank You for Listing—Letter #3

[Date]

«AddressBlock»

«GreetingLine»

I would like to say "*thank you*" for allowing me to serve you in your real estate needs. I recognize the confidence and trust you have placed in my company and me, and I assure you that I will strive to give you the best service available in our area!

I have provided information to our local Multiple Listing Service® (MLS®) organization, which will give hundreds of other real estate agents in our area access to your property. This enables not only *[Agency Name]* to try to find a buyer, but other companies as well. I do promise that I will do everything possible to qualify potential buyers before someone shows your property.

My goal is simple:

> *"To sell your home in the fastest time frame possible, with no problems, and to net you the most amount of money!"*

If at any time you would like to visit with me concerning the marketing efforts of your property, please give me a call.

As always, "*thank you*" for allowing me the opportunity to be of service to you with your real estate needs.

Sincerely,

[Agent Name]
[Agent Title]

Thank You—After Open House to Public

[Date]

«AddressBlock»

«GreetingLine»

"Thank you" for allowing me the opportunity to hold your open house this past weekend. I appreciate your getting everything ready for our open house, and the showing was excellent! I will follow up with the leads I received this weekend and keep you posted on any feedback I receive.

As always, *"thank you"* for allowing me the opportunity to be of service to you with your real estate needs, and I feel certain a SOLD sign will be here soon!

Sincerely,

[Agent Name]
[Agent Title]

[Date]

«AddressBlock»

«GreetingLine»

"Thank you" for allowing me the opportunity to hold your open house for our area real estate agents this past week. I appreciate your getting everything ready for our open house, and your home showed great! I will follow up with any more comments I receive from my colleagues and let you know of their feedback.

As always, *"thank you"* for allowing me the opportunity to be of service to you with your real estate needs, and I feel certain a SOLD sign will be here soon!

Sincerely,

[Agent Name]
[Agent Title]

Thank You for Extending Listing— Letter #1

[Date]

«AddressBlock»

«GreetingLine»

Just a note to say "*thank you*" for extending your listing with me. I appreciate your continued faith and support in me and in *[Agency Name]*. I hope that a SOLD sign will be here soon, and I want you to know that I am using every effort possible to find a buyer for your property. I realize how much a sale means to you.

Again, *thanks* for letting me serve you with your real estate needs.

Yours truly,

[Agent Name]
[Agent Title]

Thank You for Extending Listing— Letter #2

[Date]

«AddressBlock»

«GreetingLine»

Just a note to say "*thank you*" for extending your listing with me again. I appreciate your continued faith and support in me and in *[Agency Name]*. I hope that a SOLD sign will be here soon, and I want you to know that I am using every effort possible to find a buyer for your property. I realize how much a sale means to you. I have some new marketing ideas and strategies I plan to implement over the next couple of weeks, and I will keep you posted on how these new ideas develop.

Again, *thanks* for letting me serve you with your real estate needs.

Yours truly,

[Agent Name]
[Agent Title]

Thank You for Extending Listing— Letter #3

[Date]

«AddressBlock»

«GreetingLine»

Just a note to say *"thank you"* for extending your listing with me. Wow, your continued faith and support in me and in *[Agency Name]* is truly appreciated. Thank you! I feel certain a SOLD sign will be here soon, and I want you to know that I am using every effort possible to find a buyer for your property. I realize how much a sale means to you.

I will continue to implement new marketing ideas and strategies so our listing remains fresh in the consumers' and other real estate agents' eyes. I will keep you posted on how these new ideas develop, and please, always feel free to suggest or provide me with any ideas you come up with also.

Again, *thanks* for letting me serve you with your real estate needs.

Yours truly,

[Agent Name]
[Agent Title]

Thank You for Extending Listing— Letter #4

[Date]

«AddressBlock»

«GreetingLine»

Just a note to say *"thank you"* for extending your listing with me. Wow, your continued faith and support in me and in *[Agency Name]* is appreciated. Thank you!

I want you to know that I am using every effort possible to find a buyer for your property. I realize how much a sale means to you.

Please call me if you have any questions, and again, *thanks* for letting me serve you with your real estate needs.

Yours truly,

[Agent Name]
[Agent Title]

Thank You for Extending Listing— Letter #5

[Date]

«AddressBlock»

«GreetingLine»

Just a note to say "*thank you*" for extending your listing with me. You do not realize how much I appreciate your continued faith and support in me and in *[Agency Name]*. Thank you!

I want you to know that I am using every effort possible to find a buyer for your property. I realize how much a sale means to you. I will continue to implement new marketing ideas and strategies so our listing remains fresh in the consumers' and other real estate agents' eyes. I will keep you posted on how these new ideas develop, and please, always feel free to suggest or provide me with any ideas you come up with also.

Again, *thanks* for letting me serve you with your real estate needs, and I appreciate your friendship.

Yours truly,

[Agent Name]
[Agent Title]

Thank You after the Sale

[Date]

«AddressBlock»

«GreetingLine»

Just a note to say *"thank you"* for allowing me to serve you with your real estate needs. I appreciated your faith and support in me and in *[Agency Name]*. I hope that you were satisfied with my service, and please feel free to contact me with any issues or problems you might have in the future. I want you to know that I'm here to help you after the sale, and your satisfaction with my services is my top priority.

If you know of someone in the market to buy or sell, please be sure and give that person my name and telephone number. Because my business is based on commission, referrals from satisfied clients and customers mean a lot to me. If you would prefer to call me with any potential prospects, please feel free to call any time. You can also e-mail me at *[E-Mail Address]*.

Again, *thanks* for letting me serve you with your real estate needs. It was a real joy and a pleasure to work with you. Enjoy your new home!

Yours truly,

[Agent Name]
[Agent Title]

Thank You Letter—Off Market

[Date]

«AddressBlock»

«GreetingLine»

Just a note to say "*thank you*" for allowing me the opportunity to be of service to you during the time I had your property listed. My goal is to sell every listing I take, but unfortunately this doesn't always happen. I do hope my service was satisfactory, and if I can ever be of help in the future, please give me a call.

Again, *thank you*, and I wish you the best of luck!

Yours truly,

[Agent Name]
[Agent Title]

Thank You Letter—Did Not Get Listing

[Date]

«AddressBlock»

«GreetingLine»

Although I know that you have chosen another company with which to list your home for sale, I wish you the best of luck. Please keep me in mind if I can help in the future.

Again, thank you for giving me the opportunity to visit with you on your real estate needs.

Sincerely,

[Agent Name]
[Agent Title]

Listing Turned Down—Price Too High

[Date]

«AddressBlock»

«GreetingLine»

Thank you for allowing me the opportunity to preview your property this past week, and for considering my real estate services. However, I have made it a policy not to take listings that I consider to be overpriced. Turning down business is a tough decision that I must make from time to time, and, regretfully, I feel that this is one of those times. Please note that I do not hold all the answers to our local real estate activity, and yes, you might be able to sell the property for the price you want.

Please keep me in mind if you decide to re-list in the future at a lower price. I know you would appreciate my services and marketing plan, and I feel certain I could help sell your property at my recommended value. You're welcome to view my web site at [Web Address] to view current listings for sale.

Again, "*thank you*" for inviting me over to meet with you, and good luck with your marketing efforts. I do hope you understand and appreciate the basis for my decision.

Sincerely,

[Agent Name]
[Agent Title]

Vacant House Checklist Letter

[Date]

«AddressBlock»

«GreetingLine»

Enclosed you will find my monthly update form for vacant properties I currently have listed. This form will detail the items I checked for you and your property this week during my inspection. If there is something else you would like me to check during my monthly inspections, please let me know and I will be glad to include it during my visits.

As always, "*thank you*" for allowing me the opportunity to be of service to you with your real estate needs. Please feel free to call me if you ever have any questions.

Sincerely,

[Agent Name]
[Agent Title]

Fall Myth Selling Letter

[Date]

«AddressBlock»

«GreetingLine»

Is it a myth or fact? *Fall is a bad time to sell a home!* I am sure there are many excuses we could list as to why selling your property during the fall season is difficult.

- Children are back in school; so many families do not want to buy.
- The holidays are just around the corner.
- Many people are getting their homes ready for winter.
- The weather can turn bad.
- A lot of people will just wait until spring to look for a home.
- And many other excuses you have probably already thought of.

However, consider this fact. Many sellers decide to wait until February or March to list their properties, which means the number of homes for sale during the fall and winter months are minimal. This, in turn, means many buyers have fewer properties to choose from, providing your property with a higher percentage of a chance to sell. Many buyers want to relocate prior to the holiday season so they can be in their homes when family and friends come to visit.

Whether or not home sales are slower in the fall, one thing is certain: Keeping your property exposed to the market is critical to selling! Taking a break during the winter months and then re-listing in the spring when "everyone" else lists may not be a good thing after all.

I hope you will consider extending your listing with me during the fall and winter months, and I will call you in the next week to discuss this further. As always, "*thank you*" for allowing me the opportunity to be of service to you with your real estate needs. I feel certain a SOLD sign will be here soon!

Sincerely,

[Agent Name]
[Agent Title]

Post-Contract Acceptance Letter

[Date]

«AddressBlock»

«GreetingLine»

Wow, we finally did it! Although this is good news that your property is under contract, there are several additional hurdles we will need to face. I have made a short list of what happens next so that you have a good understanding of where we are and what is to come.

"Items Normally Pending at This Stage of Contract"

- Verification of Loan Documents
- Appraisal
- Inspections
- Preparation of Title Work and Escrow Documents
- Review of All Documents
- Closing

As you can see, there are still several items left to complete prior to our closing taking place. I have enclosed a "post-closing" form with the details regarding our contract and the dates by which these items must be completed.

If you have any questions during this pre-closing period of our contract, please let me know. As always, "*thank you*" for allowing me the opportunity to be of service to you with your real estate needs.

Sincerely,

[Agent Name]
[Agent Title]

Pre-Inspection Letter

[Date]

«AddressBlock»

«GreetingLine»

This *[Date of Inspection]*, *[Inspection Company]* will be conducting a general building inspection on your property. As per the sales contract, the buyers have the opportunity to conduct a building inspection on your property. This inspection will probably last for at least a couple of hours, so don't be alarmed at the length of time it will require. I always view the inspection as a protection to you and me, and it will usually helps avoid any confusion, misunderstandings, or problems that might arise after the sale.

Normally the inspector will provide a completed written report of the inspection to the buyer, detailing any concerns or issues regarding your house. Be advised that the inspector's job is "to find problems with the house." I say this so you will be prepared that any report we receive from the buyers will normally contain a lot of information. The inspector is not nit-picking; it's just his or her job to find any and all problems with the house under inspection, and to notify the buyers of these issues.

Once we are in receipt of the report we will know what items or issues the buyers would like for us to fix, if there are any requests at all. Do not become overly concerned about this until we have the inspection report in our hands, and then I can advise you on where we stand and what our position should be. In the meantime, allow the inspector free range to view your house, and be sure to answer any and all questions he or she has.

If you have any other questions about this upcoming inspection, please feel free to call me. Again, "*thank you*" for allowing me to serve you in your real estate needs. I recognize the confidence and trust you have placed in my company and me, and I value that as well as your friendship.

Sincerely,

[Agent Name]
[Agent Title]

Removal of Contingency

[Date]

«AddressBlock»

«GreetingLine»

I was informed by *[Agent or Buyer]* that the following contingency *[Contingency]* is now removed from the sales contract. This is good news, and brings us one step closer to our closing date.

Again, *thanks* for letting me serve you with your real estate needs, and I will call you with any new updates and closing details as soon as I receive them.

Yours truly,

[Agent Name]
[Agent Title]

Pre-Closing Letter

[Date]

«AddressBlock»

«GreetingLine»

We're almost there! Our closing is set for *[Closing Date]* and everything is just about complete. I have enclosed a "closing checklist" for you to review prior to moving. This checklist should cover all of the essential items that you should complete prior to turning the keys over to the new buyers.

So what happens at our closing? The buyers will sign all of their closing documents and you will sign the deed conveying title to the new owners. You will also sign a closing statement detailing your expenses for the transaction, i.e., marketing fee, taxes from January 1st until closing, any loan pay-offs, etc. As soon as I receive a copy of the settlement statement outlining these costs, I will contact you so we can proof it for accuracy.

If you have any questions prior to our closing please let me know. As always, *"thank you"* for allowing me the opportunity to be of service to you with your real estate needs.

Sincerely,

[Agent Name]
[Agent Title]

Return of Documents—
After Listing Period Ends

[Date]

«AddressBlock»

«GreetingLine»

Enclosed you will find the documents you provided me for your listing at *[Address of Property]*. I appreciate your letting me borrow these documents during the listing period. They were very helpful to our office staff and me.

As always, "*thank you*" for allowing me the opportunity to be of service to you with your real estate needs. Please let me know if I can help you in the future.

Yours truly,

[Agent Name]
[Agent Title]

Return of Documents—During Listing Period

[Date]

«AddressBlock»

«GreetingLine»

Enclosed you will find the documents you provided me for your listing at *[Address of Property]*. I appreciate your letting me borrow these documents to copy for our files to use during the listing period.

Thank you for allowing me the opportunity to be of service to you with your real estate needs. I feel certain a SOLD sign will be here soon.

Yours truly,

[Agent Name]
[Agent Title]

Moving Tips

[Date]

«AddressBlock»

«GreetingLine»

As our big day approaches for the closing, I realize you are probably beginning the huge task of packing up your belongings for your move. I have enclosed a copy of "Moving Tips" that I believe will be helpful to you during your transition. I have also enclosed a moving checklist, which is great tool to make sure you don't miss anything during this hectic time.

Again, "*thank you*" for allowing me to serve you in your real estate needs. I recognize the confidence and trust you have placed in my company and me, and I value that as well as your friendship!

Please feel free to call me if you have any questions.

Sincerely,

[Agent Name]
[Agent Title]

Asking Seller to Return Personal Property

[Date]

«AddressBlock»

«GreetingLine»

I was informed by *[Agent or Buyer]* that the following personal property was missing from the residence. I realize that this might be an oversight on your part; however, according to the sales contract you did agree to leave *[Personal Property]* with the sale of the property. If you need a copy of the sales contract showing this agreement, please let me know and I can provide you with one.

I really appreciate your business and I regret having to write you about this issue. If you have any questions regarding this matter, please don't hesitate to give me a call. I want you to know that I am here to help you after the sale, and your satisfaction with my service is my top priority.

Again, *thanks* for letting me serve you with your real estate needs. It was a real joy and a pleasure to work with you. I hope we can resolve this problem quickly.

Yours truly,

[Agent Name]
[Agent Title]

Listing Change Form Enclosure

[Date]

«AddressBlock»

«GreetingLine»

Enclosed you will find the listing status change form for your property I currently have listed. I have made the changes as we discussed by phone. Please sign this document and return it to me in the enclosed envelope so I can make the necessary changes to our files. You may also fax this document to me at [Fax Number].

As always, "*thank you*" for allowing me the opportunity to be of service to you with your real estate needs. I feel certain a SOLD sign will be here soon!

Yours truly,

[Agent Name]
[Agent Title]

Service Form Follow-Up

[Date]

«AddressBlock»

«GreetingLine»

I have enclosed a "Service Evaluation Form" for you to complete and return to me. Your participation in this survey will help me a lot. Please complete the survey and return it to *[Agency Name]* in the self-addressed stamped envelope. All submissions will be kept confidential.

At *[Agency Name]* we are always looking for ways to improve our business, and your honesty and open remarks can help us continue our quest to be the best real estate office in the area.

Again, *thanks* for letting me serve you with your real estate needs. It was a real joy and a pleasure to work with you. I hope you are enjoying your new home!

Yours truly,

[Agent Name]
[Agent Title]

Withdrawal of Listing—Letter #1

[Date]

«AddressBlock»

«GreetingLine»

This letter will serve as our agreement to end your listing contract with *[Agency Name]*. I am sorry that you wish to withdrawal your listing with our company now. My goal is to sell every listing I have, but unfortunately this does not always happen. I appreciate your business, and I hope you will consider *[Agency Name]* in the future should the need arise.

Good luck, and again, "*thank you*" for allowing *[Agency Name]* to serve you during the time we had your listing.

Sincerely,

[Agent Name]
[Agent Title]

This letter may need to come from your broker.

Withdrawal of Listing—Letter #2

[Date]

«AddressBlock»

«GreetingLine»

I am sorry that you wish to withdrawal your listing with our company and I regret that we were not able to sell it for you. My goal is to sell every listing I have, but unfortunately this does not always happen. I appreciate your business, and I hope you will consider [Agency Name] in the future should the need arise.

Good luck, and again, "*thank you*" for allowing [Agency Name] to serve you during the time we had your listing.

Sincerely,

[Agent Name]
[Agent Title]

This letter may need to come from your broker.

Letters to Other Agents and Brokers

Often, we forget the importance of communicating with our peers and colleagues. Making sure good communication lines remain open is important in this realm of our real estate industry too.

Agents will show and sell our listings, send us referrals, attend our open houses, and much more, usually to a quiet voice. Think about it for a moment. How many times have you received a note or letter for selling another real estate agent's house? Did you receive a nice thank-you note for attending one of their open houses? For showing a property another agent had listed? With *5 Minutes to a Great Real Estate Letter*, you can now avoid this trap of non-communication with your friends and colleagues, and begin thanking them for all the extra help!

Remember, *Gratitude is something of which none of us can give too much. For on the smiles, the thanks we give, our little gestures of appreciation, our neighbors build up their philosophy of life.*
— A.J. Cronin

Nice Meeting You at Class

[Date]

«AddressBlock»

«GreetingLine»

It was nice meeting you this week during our *[Class Name or Title]* in *[City]*. I hope you enjoyed the class as much as I did. Please keep me in mind for any referrals you might have for the *[Market Area]* area. I have registered your information in my address book and hope to call on you for future referrals as well.

Again, it was a real pleasure meeting you, *[Agent's First Name]*, and I hope we can visit again soon.

Sincerely,

[Agent Name]
[Agent Title]

Thanks for Writing Offer

[Date]

«AddressBlock»

«GreetingLine»

Just a note to say *"thank you"* for writing the offer on *[Address of Property]*! I'm glad we were able to get your contract accepted and I look forward to a smooth transition to our closing.

I appreciate your hard work and professionalism on this transaction, *[Agent's Name]*, and please let me know if I can help in any way through the closing date. Again, thanks!

Yours truly,

[Agent Name]
[Agent Title]

Thanks for Showing Property

[Date]

«AddressBlock»

«GreetingLine»

"Thank you" for showing my listing at *[Address of Property]* this week. I hope your showing went well, and if there is any extra information I can provide for you, please let me know.

I would like to hear any comments you and your clients have about this listing. You can return this letter with your comments to me in the enclosed, self-addressed stamped envelope, or e-mail me at *[E-Mail Address]*. You may also fax this back to me at *[Fax Number]*.

Again, "thanks" for showing my listing, *[Showing Agent's Name]*, and I hope to hear from you soon.

Yours truly,

[Agent Name]
[Agent Title]

PLEASE FEEL FREE TO WRITE YOUR COMMENTS BELOW AND RETURN IT IN THE SELF-ADDRESSED STAMPED ENVELOPE OR FAX THEM TO ME. BE SURE TO INCLUDE A RESPONSE TO THE PRICE, AND INDICATE IF YOU FEEL THE PRICE IS JUST RIGHT, TOO LOW, OR TOO HIGH. THANK YOU FOR YOUR HELP!

Thanks for Selling Property

[Date]

«AddressBlock»

«GreetingLine»

I wanted to say "*thank you*" for helping me sell *[Address of Sold House]*. I appreciate your hard work and professionalism on this transaction, *[Agent's Name]*. I hope I can return the favor for you in the near future on one of your listings. You were a joy to work with, and again, thank you for your successful efforts.

Please let me know if I can help in any way in the future.

Yours truly,

[Agent Name]
[Agent Title]

Update on Referral Offer—Listing

[Date]

«AddressBlock»

«GreetingLine»

Congratulations! I hope you will have a referral check on its way to you soon. [Seller's Name] just accepted an offer to purchase on their property I have listed. Of course, we still have several contingencies to fulfill with the contract, but I feel positive about the contract. I will keep you posted on the status of the contract and the closing date.

I am grateful for this referral, [Referring Agent's Name], and I feel it is important to keep you informed about the status of our marketing efforts. Please feel free to call me if you have any questions, and again, "thank you" for referring this listing to me.

Yours truly,

[Agent Name]
[Agent Title]

Thanks for Attending Open House

[Date]

«AddressBlock»

«GreetingLine»

I wanted to say "*thank you*" for taking time out of your busy schedule to visit my open house this past week at *[Address of Open House]*. I hope you enjoyed the tour and luncheon. If you would like to view more information about this home, you can do so at *[Web Address]*.

Again, "*thank you*" for visiting my open house, and I hope you can help locate a buyer for this listing.

Yours truly,

[Agent Name]
[Agent Title]

Thanks for Contract—Did Not Work Out

[Date]

«AddressBlock»

«GreetingLine»

"Thank you" for writing the offer on my listing at *[Address of Property]*. I am sorry that we could not work things out on your contract. I do appreciate your showing my listing and for your hard work on initiating the offer. Maybe our efforts will be more fruitful next time.

Good luck with your buyers, and please let me know if I can help in any way in the future. Again, *thanks!*

[Optional paragraph] By the way, my web site is *[Web Address]* if you want to look at the rest of my inventory in the future for other buyers you have.

Yours truly,

[Agent Name]
[Agent Title]

Thanks for Referral—After Closing

[Date]

«AddressBlock»

«GreetingLine»

Congratulations! I just closed on the *[Seller's Name]* listing you referred to me. You should receive your referral check in the next few days.

I appreciate the referral, *[Referring Agent's Name]*, and *[Seller's Name]* were a joy to work with. Please keep me in mind for any other referrals you have for my area. Again, "thank you!"

Yours truly,

[Agent Name]
[Agent Title]

Notice of Listing Price Reduction

[Date]

«AddressBlock»

«GreetingLine»

You showed my listing at *[Address of Property]* a while back, and I wanted to notify you of a price adjustment. The new listing price is *[New Price]*. I thought you might want to tell your clients of the price change if they have not bought anything at this time. I have also enclosed a new flyer for this property for you to review and keep in mind for any new clients you might have.

I appreciate any help you can offer, *[Showing Agent's Name]*. Thanks!

Yours truly,

[Agent Name]
[Agent Title]

[Date]

«AddressBlock»

«GreetingLine»

Congratulations! I hope you will have a referral check on its way to you soon. *[Buyer's Name]* found a home they liked in our area, and have an accepted contract. Of course, we still have several contingencies to fulfill with the contract, but I feel positive about the offer to purchase, and I will notify you as soon as our closing takes place.

I am grateful for this referral, *[Referring Agent's Name],* and I hope I can return the favor to you someday. Please feel free to call me if you have any questions, and again, *"thank you"* for referring *[Buyer's Name]* to me.

Yours truly,

[Agent Name]
[Agent Title]

[Date]

«AddressBlock»

«GreetingLine»

I wanted to give you an update on the referral you sent to me a while back. Unfortunately, there has not been much interest on the listing. I have contacted the *[Seller's Name]* and provided them a marketing update too. I have a couple of new marketing ideas I plan to implement for the property that I believe will increase our activity. I will keep you posted on these new updates.

I appreciate this referral, *[Referring Agent's Name],* and I wanted to keep you in the loop about the status of our marketing efforts. Please feel free to call me if you have any questions, and again, "*thank you*" for referring this listing to me.

Yours truly,

[Agent Name]
[Agent Title]

Update on Referral Offer— Need Price Reduction

[Date]

«AddressBlock»

«GreetingLine»

I wanted to give you an update on the referral you sent to me a while back. We have had several interested prospects in the property, but the general comments are that the price is too high! I have contacted *[Seller's Name]* and provided them a marketing update. Perhaps you could visit with them about adjusting the price too. I think sometimes people react more positively when someone close to them explains how pricing their real estate too high can prolong the sale of their property. I promise to keep you posted on any new updates, and I appreciate any help you can provide me on this listing to get the price adjusted.

I am grateful for this referral, *[Referring Agent's Name],* and I feel it is important to keep you informed about the status of our marketing efforts. Please feel free to call me if you have any questions, and again, *"thank you"* for referring this listing to me.

Yours truly,

[Agent Name]
[Agent Title]

Update on Referral Offer—Good Activity

[Date]

«AddressBlock»

«GreetingLine»

I wanted to give you an update on the referral you sent to me a while back. We have had several interested prospects in the property. I have contacted the *[Seller's Name]* and provided them a marketing update too. I believe we should have an offer soon based on the comments I am receiving from the other agents. I promise to keep you posted on any new updates and contracts we receive.

I appreciate this referral, *[Referring Agent's Name],* and I feel it is important to keep you informed about the status of our marketing efforts. Please feel free to call me if you have any questions, and again, *"thank you"* for referring this listing to me.

Yours truly,

[Agent Name]
[Agent Title]

Update on Referral Offer— Buyers Having No Luck

[Date]

«AddressBlock»

«GreetingLine»

I wanted to give you an update on the referral you sent to me a while back. Unfortunately, *[Buyer's Name]* have not been able to find anything that they like. We are still searching for a home that fits their needs, and I will keep you posted on any new developments that arise.

I appreciate this referral, *[Referring Agent's Name],* and I wanted you to remain in the loop about the status of our efforts. Please feel free to call me if you have any questions, and again, "*thank you*" for referring *[Buyer's Name]* to me.

Yours truly,

[Agent Name]
[Agent Title]

Letters to Vendors

Don't forget to thank the lenders, appraisers, closing agents, and other businesspeople who help you out along the way during your real estate career. Included with this book are a few letters to acknowledge your appreciation for quick responses, speaking at meetings, and more. Adding a personal touch will always set you apart from the crowd.

Please note that some of the letters included in this section are more effective if used with a handwritten note card rather than on your company letterhead. Regardless of which method you choose, it is an important tool in your real estate business.

Nice Meeting You

[Date]

«AddressBlock»

«GreetingLine»

Just a note to tell you how nice it was meeting you today. I have filed your information in my contact management program for future reference. Please keep my business card on file, too, should you require help with any real estate needs in the future.

Again, I appreciate the kindness you displayed today, and I look forward to visiting with you again soon.

Sincerely,

[Agent Name]
[Agent Title]

[Date]

«AddressBlock»

«GreetingLine»

"Thank you" for agreeing to allow *[Agency Name]* the opportunity to represent *[Name of Company]* in handling *[Name of Referrals]* for your company in *[Market Area]*. I appreciate the faith and trust you have placed in my company and me.

Again, *"thank you"* for providing me such an honor in handling your real estate needs, and please call me if you ever have any questions or concerns.

Sincerely,

[Agent Name]
[Agent Title]

Thanks for Representation—Full

[Date]

«AddressBlock»

«GreetingLine»

"Thank you" for agreeing to allow *[Agency Name]* sole representation in handling referrals for your company in *[Market Area]*. I appreciate the faith and trust you have placed in my company and me.

Again, *"thank you"* for providing me with such an honor in handling your real estate needs.

Sincerely,

[Agent Name]
[Agent Title]

Thanks to Appraiser for Quick Response

[Date]

«AddressBlock»

«GreetingLine»

Thank you for your quick response in completing the appraisal on my listing at *[Address of Property]*. I understand how busy your schedule is, and your agreement to put a rush on this appraisal will help us meet our closing date as provided in the sales contract.

Please let me know if there is anything I can assist you with in the future to make your job a little easier, *[Appraiser's Name]*. Again, *"thank you"* for your fast and professional service!

Sincerely,

[Agent Name]
[Agent Title]

[Date]

«AddressBlock»

«GreetingLine»

Thank you for rearranging your schedule to close the *[Parties to Transaction]* transaction this past week. I know this created extra work and a lot of shuffling in your schedule, and I appreciate your willingness to help us out with our situation.

Again, "*thank you*" for your help and the professional service you always extend to my clients and me!

Sincerely,

[Agent Name]
[Agent Title]

Thanks to Inspector—Quick Response

[Date]

«AddressBlock»

«GreetingLine»

Thank you for your quick response to completing the inspection on my listing at *[Address of Property]*. I understand how busy you are, and your agreement to put a rush on this inspection will help us meet our closing date as provided in the sales contract.

Please let me know if there is anything I can assist you with in the future to make your job a little easier, *[Inspector's Name]*. Again, *"thank you"* for your fast and professional service!

Sincerely,

[Agent Name]
[Agent Title]

[Date]

«AddressBlock»

«GreetingLine»

Thank you for closing our loan with *[Buyer's Name]* so quickly. Wow, my hat goes off to you!
I understand how busy you are, and your ability to close this transaction before the date in
our contract is appreciated.

I look forward to referring many more buyers to you in the future. Again, *"thank you"* for
your fast and professional service!

Sincerely,

[Agent Name]
[Agent Title]

Thanks for Speaking at Meeting

[Date]

«AddressBlock»

«GreetingLine»

It was a joy to have you speak at our *[Name of Organization]* meeting today. I appreciated your talk and learned a lot about *[Speech Topic]* that I did not know.

I realize your time is valuable. Again, *"thank you"* for contributing your time and knowledge in making our meeting such a success.

Sincerely,

[Agent Name]
[Agent Title]

Follow-Up
after the Sale

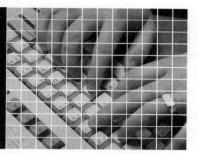

Don't throw away good business! Stay in contact with your past clients and customers so they will use your real estate services in the future! According to the *National Association of REALTORS® Profile of Home Buyers and Sellers*, only 20 percent of repeat buyers used the same agent as before. From this research, it is evident that many agents are not doing a good job in following-up with their clients long after the sale.

Having a consistent client reminder program is important if you plan to reap future profits from past customers and clients. Included in this section is a wide variety of letters to help you accomplish this task.

First-Year Anniversary Letter

[Date]

«AddressBlock»

«GreetingLine»

Happy Anniversary!

Can you believe it's been one full year since the purchase of your home? Wow, time does go by quickly. I hope that your home has been a joy to you and your family this past year, and that it is still the ideal place for you to enjoy and grow into for many years to come. I also hope that you will continue to keep my name and business card available for anyone you know looking to buy or sell real estate. I often remind friends and family members how much my business depends on referrals from friends like you. I have enclosed several business cards for you to hand out should you know of someone interested in buying or selling real estate.

Again, *Happy Anniversary* on the purchase of your home, and please know that I am here long after the sale for any needs you might have.

Sincerely,

[Agent Name]
[Agent Title]

Second-Year Anniversary Letter

[Date]

«AddressBlock»

«GreetingLine»

Happy Anniversary!

Yes, it's now two years since you bought your home. I'm sure your home is fulfilling your family's needs, and is a place you can call home. The real joy and satisfaction I receive with my career is helping families like yours find a home they can enjoy for many years.

Again, *Happy Anniversary* on the purchase of your home, and please know that I am here long after the sale for any needs you might have.

Sincerely,

[Agent Name]
[Agent Title]

Third-Year Anniversary Letter

[Date]

«AddressBlock»

«GreetingLine»

Happy Anniversary!

Yes, it's been three years since you purchased your home from me. I hope your home is fulfilling your family's needs, and is a place you can all call home. If you need more room, or have a desire to relocate in the near future, please let me know. I would love to help you on your next real estate transaction. Now is a great time to buy and sell. Call me for information on today's real estate market.

Again, *Happy Anniversary* on the purchase of your home, and please know that I am here long after the sale for any needs you might have.

Sincerely,

[Agent Name]
[Agent Title]

Fourth-Year Anniversary Letter

[Date]

«AddressBlock»

«GreetingLine»

Happy Anniversary!

Wow, can you believe it was four years ago you bought your home? I'm sure you've added and changed many items within your home, and I hope it is still fulfilling all of your needs. I appreciated the opportunity to work with you on your home buy, and I hope all is going well with you.

Again, *Happy Anniversary* on the purchase of your home, and let me know if I can help in the future. Thanks!

Sincerely,

[Agent Name]
[Agent Title]

Fifth-Year Anniversary Letter

[Date]

«AddressBlock»

«GreetingLine»

Happy Anniversary!

Five years ago we closed on your house purchase. Wow, time goes by quickly! I appreciated the opportunity to work with you on your home buy, and I hope all is going well with you.

Again, *Happy Anniversary* on the purchase of your home, and let me know if I can help in the future. Thanks!

Sincerely,

[Agent Name]
[Agent Title]

Sixth-Year Anniversary Letter

[Date]

«AddressBlock»

«GreetingLine»

Happy Anniversary!

There are two parts of my business that are rewarding to me. The first is a satisfied client who uses my services or recommends me to friends for their real estate needs. The second gratifying aspect of my business is when past clients purchase a home they enjoy and stay there for a long time. Congratulations! This is the sixth-year anniversary of your home buy. I know I have said this in previous letters, but time does go by quickly! I appreciated the opportunity to work with you on your home buy six years ago, and I hope all is going well with you.

Again, *Happy Anniversary* on the purchase of your home, and let me know if I can help in the future. Thanks!

Sincerely,

[Agent Name]
[Agent Title]

Seventh-Year Anniversary Letter

[Date]

«AddressBlock»

«GreetingLine»

Happy Anniversary!

It's time for my annual congratulations letter, and this is year number seven! I know I mention this every year, but time does go by quickly! It seems like yesterday that we closed on your home purchase. I am so glad you are still enjoying your home. If you would like to have an updated price evaluation on the equity in your home based on the current market conditions, I would be glad to do that for you. There's no charge, and it does not take long to complete. I appreciated the opportunity to work with you seven years ago on your home buy, and I hope all is going well with you.

Again, *Happy Anniversary* on the purchase of your home, and let me know if I can help in the future. Thanks!

Sincerely,

[Agent Name]
[Agent Title]

Recently Sold Home in Your Neighborhood

[Date]

«AddressBlock»

«GreetingLine»

Hello! I hope all is well with you and your family. I wanted to let you know I recently sold a home in your neighborhood. From this current transaction, it looks as though your real estate buy was a good investment. Real estate values in your neighborhood are on the rise. If you would like to know what the estimated market value is for the home you bought through me, please give me a call. I'll be glad to research this information for you, and best of all it's FREE!

Again, I hope you and your family are doing well, and please keep me in mind for any future real estate needs.

Sincerely,

[Agent Name]
[Agent Title]

Compliment on Condition of House

[Date]

«AddressBlock»

«GreetingLine»

I was by your house recently on an appointment and noticed how nice everything looked. You are taking great pride in your real estate ownership, and it shows! It's exciting to see homes like yours in such excellent condition after the sale. I hope you are enjoying your home, and I hope you have many great years of memories there.

It was an honor to represent you on your real estate transaction, and feel free to call me any time you have a question or real estate need.

Sincerely,

[Agent Name]
[Agent Title]

Forwarding Tax Statement after First Year

[Date]

«AddressBlock»

«GreetingLine»

I hope your holidays were joyous, and the New Year is off to a great start. I know that you will be preparing your tax returns during the next few months, so I have enclosed a copy of your settlement statement from this past year. Don't forget that there are many good tax-deductible items on this statement that you may be able to use this year when preparing your return. Please be sure to consult your tax advisor for more information about which closing costs are permissible for consideration on your taxes.

As always, I appreciate your business, and please feel free to call me any time with your real estate questions.

Sincerely,

[Agent Name]
[Agent Title]

Public Relations Letters

For many people, "tooting" their own horn is hard to do. But let's face it, if you don't promote yourself, no one else will. It's important to make sure you keep your name in the public eye, so that when people think of real estate, they think of you!

As Ralph Waldo Emerson said, *"If I cannot brag of knowing something, then I brag of not knowing it; at any rate, brag."*

It's important to remember that you're not the only real estate agent in your community vying for the customer's business. If you don't promote yourself, someone else will promote himself or herself, and that's who will likely win the business.

Agent—When Changing Companies

[Date]

«AddressBlock»

«GreetingLine»

I have some exciting news that I wanted to share with you about my real estate career. I am now associated with *[New Agency Name]*. This move will offer me many new opportunities as a real estate professional. I believe it will also benefit my current and past clients and customers.

I have enclosed my new business card for your future reference. Please call me for any real estate needs you have. You can still access my web page at *[Web Address]* to search local listings and get timely real estate information.

I appreciate your friendship, *[Letter Name],* and I hope you will continue to support me at *[New Agency Name]*. Thank you!

Sincerely,

[Agent Name]
[Agent Title]

Completion of Real Estate Course— Letter #1

[Date]

«AddressBlock»

«GreetingLine»

Recently I completed *[Name of Class]*. This class dealt primarily with *[Type of Class]* issues in our real estate industry. I have a commitment to maintain an involvement with my real estate profession, and to furthering my knowledge in this business I enjoy so much. Most of all, I want you to know that I take educational classes for clients like you, so that when a need arises, you know you can count on me to be ready and prepared to help.

I appreciate your friendship, and if you know of someone in the market to buy or sell a home please give him or her my card. Don't forget, you can visit my web site at *[Web Address]* to view homes for sale in our area and find good real estate information.

My business is dependent on referrals and support from people like you, *[Letter Name]*. Thanks!

Sincerely,

[Agent Name]
[Agent Title]

Completion of Real Estate Course— Letter #2

[Date]

«AddressBlock»

«GreetingLine»

I wanted to write you a short note and tell you about a new real estate course I just completed, *[Name of Course]*. I continue to take real estate educational courses as often as possible so I can stay ahead of the many changes in my industry. More importantly, I know that when it comes time to help friends like you with your real estate needs, I can give you the professional service you deserve.

I hope everything is going well for you, and please let me know if I can help with any real estate needs in the future.

By the way, my web site address is *[Web Address]*. The site offers good information for buying and selling real estate, as well as the capability to search listings currently for sale. Thanks for your time!

Sincerely,

[Agent Name]
[Agent Title]

New Agent Introductory Letter

[Date]

«AddressBlock»

«GreetingLine»

I wanted to write you a brief note and tell you some exciting news about my career change. I am now working as a real estate professional for *[Agency Name]*. After several weeks in real estate school, passing the appropriate exams, and completing my company sales training, I am now ready to help with your real estate needs.

Please feel free to contact me with any of your real estate requests. Also, please keep me in mind if you know of someone who is interested in buying or selling real estate. One of my biggest needs is referrals of customers from friends like you.

Finally, I have a web site address you can visit at *[Web Address – Company or Personal]*. This web site offers the opportunity for your property to be marketed 24 hours a day, 7 days a week! According to the *2003 National Association of REALTORS® Profile of Home Buyers and Sellers,* 65 percent of consumers used the Internet as a source to find homes to buy. At *[Agency Name]*, we can offer you this type of service, and much more!

I appreciate your friendship, and I hope to help you or your friends with your real estate needs soon.

Sincerely,

[Agent Name]
[Agent Title]

New Agent Introductory Letter from Broker #1

[Date]

«AddressBlock»

«GreetingLine»

[Agency Name] is pleased to announce the affiliation of *[Agent's Name]* to our company. *[Agent's Name]* has just completed an extensive training course to complete and pass the state licensing exam. *[Agency Name]* has also provided a detailed training program for *[Agent's Name]*, and *[he/she]* is now ready to serve you with your real estate needs.

[Agency Name] has been helping families with their real estate needs since *[Year Agency Opened]*. You can visit our web site at *[Web Address]* and find out more information about *[Agency Name]*.

I hope you will consider *[Agent's Name]* for all of your real estate needs. Also, encourage any friends, family members, or co-workers to consider *[Agent's Name]* for their real estate needs too.

"Thank you" for your time, and I hope *[Agent's Name]* will hear from you soon.

Yours truly,

[Agent Name]
[Agent Title]

New Agent Introductory Letter from Broker #2

[Date]

«AddressBlock»

«GreetingLine»

[Agency Name] is proud to announce the affiliation of *[Agent's Name]* to our staff. *[Agent's Name]* has just completed all of the necessary requirements by *[State]* to receive *[his/her]* license, and we are excited to have *[him/her]* be a part of our team.

I hope you will consider using *[Agent's Name]* for any future real estate needs, and allow *[him/her]* the opportunity to show you *[Agency Name]*'s aggressive marketing plan.

For a complete listing of homes for sale and other information about *[Agency Name],* visit our web site at *[Web Address].*

"Thank you" for your time, and I hope *[Agent's Name]* will hear from you soon.

Yours truly,

[Agent Name]
[Agent Title]

Congratulations on Job Promotion

[Date]

«AddressBlock»

«GreetingLine»

Congratulations on your recent job promotion! I know you will be excellent in this new position, and your company picked the right person. This is a great honor, and I know you are excited and proud of the new challenge.

Good luck with your new role, and again, congratulations!

Sincerely,

[Agent Name]
[Agent Title]

Congratulations on Birth of Child

[Date]

«AddressBlock»

«GreetingLine»

Congratulations on the new addition to your family! I know you are thrilled about the birth of your child, and the exciting days that lay ahead for you. Don't worry, you'll do just fine, and I could not think of anyone else who would make such fine parents.

Again, congratulations, Mom and Dad!

Sincerely,

[Agent Name]
[Agent Title]

Thank You for Recommending Clients

[Date]

«AddressBlock»

«GreetingLine»

Thank you for providing me such a wonderful letter of recommendation to use with my marketing materials. I appreciate your help, and the letter was exceptional. Thank you!

I hope all is going well with you and your family, and I hope you are settled in with your new move. Let me know if I can help with any real estate needs in the future, and don't forget to mention my name when you hear of someone interested in buying or selling real estate.

Thanks again.

Sincerely,

[Agent Name]
[Agent Title]

Referral Letters

The following section contains a selection of letters to acknowledge and thank recipients for referrals given to you during the course of your real estate career. You will also find a few letters to notify agents about the status of their referrals placed with you and your company.

Thanks to Friend for Referral

[Date]

«AddressBlock»

«GreetingLine»

"*Thank you*" for the recent referral you provided me. I appreciate your help and support with my business, and yes, referrals are an important part of my continued success in the real estate industry. Please know that I will give *[Client's Name]* the utmost care and professionalism with *[his/her]* real estate transaction.

Again, "*thank you*" for the referral *[Letter Name]*.

Sincerely,

[Agent Name]
[Agent Title]

Thanks to Friend for Referral after Sale

[Date]

«AddressBlock»

«GreetingLine»

Just a note to let you know that I recently closed with *[Clients' Name]* on their real estate transaction and to again say *"thank you"* for the referral! I appreciate your help and support with my business. Referrals are such an important part of my continued success in the real estate industry, and it's people like you, *[Letter Name],* who help make this all possible.

Again, *"thank you"* for the referral!

Sincerely,

[Agent Name]
[Agent Title]

Thanks—Buyers Chose Other Area

[Date]

«AddressBlock»

«GreetingLine»

This letter will serve as an official update as to the status of *[Name of Referred Client]*. As of today, *[Insert Date]*, *[Clients' Name]* have not purchased anything from our company. They have decided to look in another area, and are no longer actively working with *[Agency Name]*. If something changes I will keep you informed.

Thank you so much for the referral, and please keep me in mind in the future for any referrals you have in the *[Market Area]*. Again, "*thank you*!"

Yours truly,

[Agent Name]
[Agent Title]

Thanks to Friend— Listing Referral Did Not Work

[Date]

«AddressBlock»

«GreetingLine»

Thank you for the listing referral with *[Clients' Name]*. Unfortunately, *[he/she/they]* chose another real estate firm to list with. I am sorry I was not able to help your friends now, but maybe I can assist them in the future should the need arise.

Again, "thanks" for providing me with this listing referral lead. I appreciate your thinking of me.

Sincerely,

[Agent Name]
[Agent Title]

[Date]

«AddressBlock»

«GreetingLine»

"Thank you" for the recent referral you provided me. Unfortunately, *[Clients' Name]* are already working with another agent. I appreciate your help and support with my business, and yes, referrals are an important part of my continued success in the real estate industry.

Please keep me in mind for future referral leads you meet. Again, thank you!

Sincerely,

[Agent Name]
[Agent Title]

Letters from Brokers

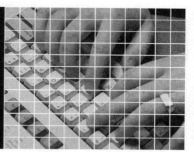

There are two letters in this section for specific use by brokers, although many of the letters found elsewhere can easily be tailored and used by the company. There are also a few additional letters on the resource CD-ROM for brokers.

[Date]

«AddressBlock»

«GreetingLine»

I believe you would make an excellent candidate for a career in real estate. A real estate career is a rewarding opportunity that offers an excellent compensation package for those willing to work hard. It also provides a flexible work schedule for you and your family.

I would be happy to visit with you in more detail about this exciting career challenge. Feel free to contact me at *[Phone Number]* for more information. Thank you for your time, and I hope you will consider real estate as a possible new profession.

Yours truly,

[Agent Name]
[Agent Title]

Follow-Up on Interest in Real Estate Career

[Date]

«AddressBlock»

«GreetingLine»

It was nice meeting you this week and discussing a possible career in real estate with *[Agency Name]*. I believe you would make an excellent real estate agent, and I would love to have you join our team.

Please feel free to call me if you have any more questions about the real estate profession, and I will contact you as soon as I have information and dates for the next real estate school. Again, it was a pleasure meeting you.

Sincerely,

[Agent Name]
[Agent Title]

E-Mail Messages

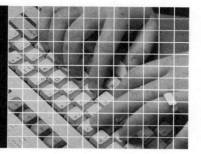

In today's fast-paced society, communicating with our friends, family members, co-workers, and clients is a whole new world. In just the last ten years, cellular telephones have overtaken the majority of our lives, and the 2004 National Association of REALTORS® Technology Impact Survey shows that 95 percent of REALTORS® own cell phones. This same study reveals that 24 percent use e-mail on a regular basis for communicating with their clients.

Because all of us have different personalities, some clients will prefer that you stay in contact with them by e-mail instead of standard U.S. postal mail. I caution you to use e-mail sparingly, and avoid using e-mail for controversial issues. If you have difficulty explaining your point to the reader as you write your e-mail, it's probably not a good idea to use this method of communication. Pick up the telephone or, if applicable, make a personal visit. Still, there are times when e-mail is effective. Using e-mail to point a client or customer to a property's web address link or your web site is an excellent way to accomplish this task. E-mail is also a quick, efficient, and inexpensive way to let prospects and other agents know of price reductions, new listings, and other timely information.

Sometimes, having standard wording you can copy and paste into your e-mail message is ideal when you are short on time and need to provide the same information to each recipient. For those tasks, I believe you will find many of the e-mail messages in this book helpful. Additional e-mail messages are located on the resource CD-ROM, along with scenarios showing you how to use these e-mail messages quickly and effectively.

«GreetingLine»

"Thank you" for allowing me to visit with you about the real estate you are selling.   I appreciated the kindness and hospitality you showed, and I wish you the best of luck regarding your home sale. Please feel free to call me if you have a concern or question that you would like to discuss.

I have provided a link to the environmental protection agency so that you can download a lead-based paint disclosure. You can find these forms at http://www.epa.gov, and search for lead-based paint disclosure. If you have problems finding this form, please call me and I will be glad to print out one for you. Remember, if your home was built before October 1978, additional rules apply, and you need to provide this form to any prospective buyers.

Again, *"thanks"* for being so kind and generous during my visit. Good luck, and please let me know if I can help in any way.

Sincerely,

[Agent Name]
[Agent Title]
[Web Address]
Mailto: [E-Mail Address]
[Phone] – [Fax]
Licensed to practice real estate in [State]
[Quote or Slogan]

Buyer Stopping by Office

«GreetingLine»

"Thank you" for stopping by my real estate office this past week. I realize home ownership is a big decision for you, and that you might still have many questions. I found an interesting link on the Internet called "100 Questions & Answers About Buying A New Home" on the HUD web site. You can view this information from the link above. Please note that if the link does not work for some reason, you can still go the HUD main web site and search under information for buyers. The HUD web site is http://www.hud.gov.

As always, *"thank you"* for allowing me the opportunity to be of service to you with your real estate needs, and I hope you find this information helpful.

Sincerely,

[Agent Name]
[Agent Title]
[Web Address]
Mailto: [E-Mail Address]
[Phone] – [Fax]
Licensed to practice real estate in [State]
[Quote or Slogan]

«GreetingLine»

Thank you so much for the e-mail. I have attached a link below for you to preview this listing. If you would like more information or would like to arrange an appointment to preview this home, please give me a call.

Would you like to be the first to hear about new listings that might interest you? If so, reply to this message and give me a brief description as to what you are looking for. I can set up a special search for you in our MLS® so any new listings will go directly to your e-mail. Please keep in mind that some of the listings might be with another real estate firm; however, you can still put my real estate experience to work for you. Just call me so I can take care of all the needed details.

Again, thanks for the e-mail and I hope to hear from you soon.

[Link to Property]

Sincerely,

[Agent Name]
[Agent Title]
[Web Address]
Mailto: [E-Mail Address]
[Phone] – [Fax]
Licensed to practice real estate in [State]
[Quote or Slogan]

«GreetingLine»

Thank you so much for the e-mail. I have attached a link below for you to preview this commercial listing. If you would like more information or would like to arrange an appointment to preview this property please give me a call.

Would you like to be the first to hear about new listings that might interest you? If so, reply to this message and give me a brief description as to what commercial property you are looking for. I can set up a special search for you in our MLS® so any new listings will go directly to your e-mail. Please keep in mind that some of the listings might be with another real estate firm; however, you can still put my real estate experience to work for you.

Again, thanks for the e-mail and I hope to hear from you soon.

[Link to Property]

Sincerely,

[Agent Name]
[Agent Title]
[Web Address]
Mailto: [E-Mail Address]
[Phone] – [Fax]
Licensed to practice real estate in [State]
[Quote or Slogan]

Buyer Inquiry—Land

«GreetingLine»

Thank you so much for the e-mail. I have attached a link below for you to preview this land listing. If you would like more information or would like a plat of the property please let me know.

Would you like to be the first to hear about new land listings that might interest you? If so, reply to this message and give me a brief description as to how many acres you are looking for and the area you would prefer. Indicate also if you would like wooded or cleared land. Just give me your land "wish list," and I can set up a special search for you in our MLS® so any new listings will go directly to your e-mail. Keep in mind that some of the listings might be with another real estate firm, but you can still put my real estate experience to work for you.

Again, thanks for the e-mail!

[Link to Property]

Sincerely,

[Agent Name]
[Agent Title]
[Web Address]
Mailto: [E-Mail Address]
[Phone] – [Fax]
Licensed to practice real estate in [State]
[Quote or Slogan]

Buyer Inquiry—Building Lot

«GreetingLine»

Thank you so much for the e-mail. I have attached a link below for you to preview this lot listing. If you would like more information or would like a plat of the property please let me know.

Would you like to be the first to hear about new building lot listings that might interest you? If so, reply to this message and give me a brief description as to what you are looking for and the area you would prefer. I can set up a special search for you in our MLS® so any new listings will go directly to your e-mail. Keep in mind that some of the listings might be with another real estate firm, but you can still put my real estate experience to work for you.

Again, thanks for the e-mail!

[Link to Property]

Sincerely,

[Agent Name]
[Agent Title]
[Web Address]
Mailto: *[E-Mail Address]*
[Phone] – [Fax]
Licensed to practice real estate in [State]
[Quote or Slogan]

«GreetingLine»

I hope things are going well for you! I wanted to let you know that the property I showed you at *[Address of Property]* was just reduced to *[New Price]*. If you still have an interest in this property, please let me know. If you would like to preview the property again, I can arrange an appointment. Provided below is a link to the listing if you would like to read more about it.

As always, "*thank you*" for allowing me the opportunity to be of service to you with your real estate needs, and I hope to hear from you soon.

[Link to Property]

Sincerely,

[Agent Name]
[Agent Title]
[Web Address]
Mailto: [E-Mail Address]
[Phone] – [Fax]
Licensed to practice real estate in [State]
[Quote or Slogan]

«GreetingLine»

Well, it's our first week of marketing your real estate, and I wanted to update you on what has occurred and will occur early on during this listing period. I have detailed a few of our marketing endeavors below:

- Property information put in our local Multiple Listing Service® (MLS®).
- Property information sent to *[Web Address]*, as well as added to web sites *[Agency Name]* uses.
- Digital photos taken and uploaded to the proper web sites and MLS®.
- Letters and/or e-mails sent to top agents in our area announcing your property for sale.
- Open house scheduled for *[Date of Open House]*.
- Agent tour completed. Evaluations and comments were positive!
- Flyers prepared for distribution to potential customers.
- *[List other items Completed Here]*

Naturally, there is much behind-the-scenes work done daily to market and sell your property of which you may not be aware or we have not listed. The important point to know is that I am busy trying to sell your house, and I want your total satisfaction in my services. If at any time you have questions, give me a call.

I do appreciate your business and I hope that a SOLD sign will be here soon! Please feel free to call me if you ever have any questions, and again, *"thank you"* for your business.

Yours truly,

[Agent Name]
[Agent Title]
[Web Address]
Mailto: [E-Mail Address]
[Phone] – [Fax]
Licensed to practice real estate in [State]
[Quote or Slogan]

Web Address Link for Sellers

«GreetingLine»

Your listing is now on the World Wide Web. Here is the link from our company web site to preview your listing.

[Link to Listing]

I hope the listing information meets with your approval. Please keep in mind that we're limited to the type and amount of information we can list on the Internet. If there is anything you would like to discuss with me about the information listed, please give me a call.

Again, thanks for placing your confidence in me, and I look forward in providing a SOLD sign to you soon!

Sincerely,

[Agent Name]
[Agent Title]
[Web Address]
Mailto: [E-Mail Address]
[Phone] – [Fax]
Licensed to practice real estate in [State]
[Quote or Slogan]

Thank You E-Mail—Sellers

«GreetingLine»

"Thank you" for listing your real estate with me today. I am preparing the necessary documents for our Multiple Listing Service® and Internet web sites. Once I have everything uploaded to the Internet, I will send you a web address link so you can preview the listing and let me know if there are any corrections I should make.

Again, thanks for placing your confidence in me, and I look forward in providing a SOLD sign to you soon!

Sincerely,

[Agent Name]
[Agent Title]
[Web Address]
Mailto: [E-Mail Address]
[Phone] – [Fax]
Licensed to practice real estate in [State]
[Quote or Slogan]

Agent Tour Follow-Up to Sellers

«GreetingLine»

Just a note to tell you *"thanks"* for allowing our office to tour your real estate listing this week. Each week our office tours new listings to help our agents become more familiar with our inventory for upcoming property calls. We also ask the agents to fill out evaluation sheets indicating their thoughts on price, marketability features, and anything we might do to improve the salability of the property. I will call you this week to go over the evaluation sheets for your property.

I do appreciate your business and I hope that a SOLD sign will be here soon! Please feel free to call me if you ever have any questions, and again *"thank you"* for your business.

Yours truly,

[Agent Name]
[Agent Title]
[Web Address]
Mailto: [E-Mail Address]
[Phone] – [Fax]
Licensed to practice real estate in [State]
[Quote or Slogan]

Home Warranty Offer to Sellers

«GreetingLine»

I wanted to tell you about a marketing idea that could stimulate more interest in your property. Many times a seller will offer a home warranty program to the new buyer as a marketing incentive. This is an excellent feature that covers many problems that can occur after the closing. This warranty gives the buyer peace of mind that if something does break down or go wrong, he or she may have insurance to cover it. I have information I can send you if this sounds like something you might want to include with the sale of your house. Keep in mind that there is no obligation to do this, it's just a suggestion to help with marketing your real estate.

[Optional: Link to Home Warranty Web Site, if Available]

I do appreciate your business and I hope that a SOLD sign will be here soon! Please feel free to call me if you ever have any questions, and again *"thank you"* for your business.

Yours truly,

[Agent Name]
[Agent Title]
[Web Address]
Mailto: [E-Mail Address]
[Phone] – [Fax]
Licensed to practice real estate in [State]
[Quote or Slogan]

Pre-Closing Note to Sellers

«GreetingLine»

We're almost there! Our closing is set for *[Closing Date]* and everything is just about complete.

So what happens at our closing? The buyers will sign all of their closing documents, and you will sign the deed conveying title to the new owners. You will also sign a closing statement detailing your expenses for the transaction, i.e., marketing fee, taxes from January 1 until closing, any loan pay-offs, etc. As soon as I receive a copy of the settlement statement outlining these costs, I will contact you so we can proof it for accuracy prior to closing.

I do appreciate your business! Please feel free to call me if you ever have any questions, and again "*thank you*" for your business.

Yours truly,

[Agent Name]
[Agent Title]
[Web Address]
Mailto: [E-Mail Address]
[Phone] – [Fax]
Licensed to practice real estate in [State]
[Quote or Slogan]

Property Back on Market—To Agents

«GreetingLine»

I wanted to let you know that the property I had listed at *[Address of Property]* is back on the market. If you know of someone interested in this property, I can arrange an appointment for you and your client. Provided below is a link to the listing if you would like to read more about it.

Thanks for your time, and I hope you can help me sell this property.

[Link to Listing]

Sincerely,

[Agent Name]
[Agent Title]
[Web Address]
Mailto: [E-Mail Address]
[Phone] – [Fax]
Licensed to practice real estate in [State]
[Quote or Slogan]

Price Reduction—Agents

«GreetingLine»

I wanted to let you know that the property I have listed at *[Address of Property]* was just reduced to *[New Price]*. If you know of someone interested in this property, I can arrange an appointment for you. Provided below is a link to the listing if you would like to read more about it.

Thanks for your time, and I hope you can help me sell this property.

[Link to Listing]

Sincerely,

[Agent Name]
[Agent Title]
[Web Address]
Mailto: [E-Mail Address]
[Phone] – [Fax]
Licensed to practice real estate in [State]
[Quote or Slogan]

E-Mail Messages

Thanks for Selling Property—Agents

«GreetingLine»

"Thank you" for selling my listing at *[Address of Property]*. I appreciated your hard work and your professionalism on this transaction, and I hope I can return the favor to you someday.

Again, *"thank you,"* *[Selling Agent],* for selling my listing! You did a great job!

Sincerely,

[Agent Name]
[Agent Title]
[Web Address]
Mailto: [E-Mail Address]
[Phone] – [Fax]
Licensed to practice real estate in [State]
[Quote or Slogan]

«GreetingLine»

"Thank you" for showing my listing at *[Property Address]* on *[Date of Showing]*. I hope the showing went well, and I am eager to hear any feedback on what your buyers thought of the property. Please reply to this message and let me know what the comments were so I can provide them to my clients.

Again, *"thank you,"* *[Showing Agent],* for showing my listing, and I hope I hear from you soon. Let me know if there is anything else I can do.

Yours truly,

[Agent Name]
[Agent Title]
[Web Address]
Mailto: [E-Mail Address]
[Phone] – [Fax]
Licensed to practice real estate in [State]
[Quote or Slogan]

«GreetingLine»

Just a note to tell you how nice it was meeting you today. I have filed your information in my contact management program for future reference. Please keep my name on file, too, should you require help with any real estate needs in the future.

Again, I appreciate the kindness you displayed today, and I look forward to visiting with you again soon.

Sincerely,

[Agent Name]
[Agent Title]
[Web Address]
Mailto: [E-Mail Address]
[Phone] – [Fax]
Licensed to practice real estate in [State]
[Quote or Slogan]

Thanks to Loan Officer—Vendor E-Mail

«GreetingLine»

Thank you for closing our loan with *[Buyer's Name]* so quickly. Wow, my hat goes off to you!
I understand how busy you are, and your ability to close this transaction before the date in
our contract is appreciated.

I look forward to referring many more buyers to you in the future. Again, *"thank you"* for
your fast and professional service!

Sincerely,

[Agent Name]
[Agent Title]
[Web Address]
Mailto: [E-Mail Address]
[Phone] – [Fax]
Licensed to practice real estate in [State]
[Quote or Slogan]

New in Real Estate Business—E-Mail

«GreetingLine»

Just a quick note to tell you that I am now affiliated with *[Agency Name]*. You can visit our web site at *[Web Address]*. *[Agency Name]* has been helping families with their real estate needs and is a name you can trust. Before you buy or sell a home or, before a friend or family member buys or sells a home, call me for any real estate needs. My direct phone number is *[Phone Number]*.

Thanks for your time, and I hope to hear from you soon!

[Optional] Would you like to receive one of the following? If so, click on the link below and send your e-mail request. I'll reply to you as quickly as possible with the information.

Avoid the 10 Biggest Mistakes in Selling a Home.
How to Save Thousands of Dollars on Your Next Home Purchase.

Sincerely,

[Agent Name]
[Agent Title]
[Web Address]
Mailto: [E-Mail Address]
[Phone] – [Fax]
Licensed to practice real estate in [State]
[Quote or Slogan]

See the viewlet called "Add Your Name to E-mails" on the CD-ROM for instructions on how to insert your e-mail address into the e-mail links above.

Fax Templates

I often find myself needing to send a quick fax to a client or another agent regarding a contract or counteroffer. This task usually comes when there is not a lot of extra time. I felt it would be great to include a few facsimile templates for you to use in these situations. I have included two templates in the book for you to preview, and several more on the resource CD-ROM. I hope you find the templates a great time saver and let them help you present a more professional look with this form of communication.

Fax Cover Sheet—For Counteroffer

Fax transmittal

From *[Agent Name]*
[Agent Phone]
[Agent Fax]
[E-Mail]
[Web Address]
[Date]

To: _____

Fax #: _____

Phone #: _____

RE: _____

Number of Pages: _____

The following facsimile contains the documents for the counteroffer for the property at *[Property Address]*. Please sign and/or initial each page where indicated and return to me at the above fax number. If you have any questions, please do not hesitate to give me a call.

As always, "thank you" for allowing me the opportunity to be of service to you with your real estate needs.

Yours truly,

[Agent Name]
[Agent Title]

Fax Cover Sheet—For Appraiser

Fax transmittal

From [Agent Name]
[Agent Phone]
[Agent Fax]
[E-Mail]
[Web Address]
[Date]

To: _____

Fax #: _____

Phone #: _____

RE: _____

Number of Pages: _____

The following facsimile contains the documents you requested for the property you're appraising at *[Property Address]*. Please let me know if there is anything else that you need to complete this appraisal. For your information, I have included some important dates we must meet to remain in compliance with this transaction.

Date for closing _____

Date appraisal needed _____

Contact name and phone number for this file _____

_____

As always, "thank you" for your prompt and professional attention.

Yours truly,

[Agent Name]
[Agent Title]

Fax Templates

Conclusion

As I think back on my real estate career, I am grateful for two important classes I took in my school days. The first is my typing class in the tenth grade. I am very thankful for having Mrs. Mary Lee Faircloth, who was such a good teacher in this class. I often wondered why our school required typing to graduate, but it didn't take long to figure out how important this class was when I entered the business world.

I'm also indebted to a class entitled "Business Correspondence and Reports" I took at Southeast Missouri State University in Cape Girardeau, Missouri. It was a great class, and those letters and reports I had to do for my instructor each day helped to shape and mold the beginning of a long and profitable real estate career. I can honestly say that I won more listings over competing agents in my area because I knew how to put together a good looking report that impressed the customer. I also discovered the value and importance of thanking the client, and keeping in close contact with my friends during and after my business with them. I hope you will use these letters and find the same success I found in communicating with people.

As Dale Carnegie said so long ago in his best-selling book, *How to Win Friends and Influence People,* "You can make more friends in two months by becoming genuinely interested in other people than you can in two years by trying to get other people interested in you." By staying in touch, whether by telephone, e-mail, personal visit, or a card or letter, you demonstrate your desire to become interested in others.

When you can do that with a sincere and honest passion, there's no telling how far your professional career will soar.

Best of luck!

John D. Mayfield